JOHN OGILVIE entered the religious congregation of the Marist Brothers in 1938 at the age of eighteen.

St Marcellin Champagnat, a priest, founded the congregation in 1817, two years after the Treaty of Vienna which marked the close of the Napoleonic wars. His consuming desire was to provide the key element of education for poor children on the fringes of society the world over. He wished to affirm, confirm and promote their spiritual and cultural growth under the protection of the Virgin Mary to open up for them the joy of a fully integrated adulthood in Jesus Christ.

In 1858, the Marist Brothers came to Glasgow and set up a school, which later became St Mungo's Academy. Thirty years later, in 1888, Brother Walfrid founded Celtic Football Club to raise money to provide school meals for the poor children from the east end of the city.

Having graduated from the University of Glasgow with and Honour's degree in English language and literature, John Ogilvie became engaged in school work in St Chad's College, Wolverhampton; the Rosary School, Birmingham; St Mark's JS; thirteen years in St Mungo's Academy and finally as head of St Andrew's Secondary in the east end of Glasgow for fifteen years.

During a period of twenty-five years he took charge of school summer camps in Elgin, Hopeman, Lossiemouth and Nairn in the north of Scotland.

Bob Horne, a teacher who had been at school with the Benedictines used to say that 'the Marist Brothers were the poor man's Benedictine.'

John Ogilvie spent five years as an assistant in St Joseph's Church, Bunhill Row near the Barbican and then five years in Cameroon, West Africa.

The Marist Brothers, ennobled with their martyrs in China, Africa and Spain, are experiencing a shift in focus from their apostolate in western Europe to the Far East, India, Pakistan and China.

The future is bright and full of promise. The harvest is rich and the Lord is with us.

Feasts of
the Blessed
Virgin Mary

Feasts of the Blessed Virgin Mary

Marist Brother
John Ogilvie, F.M.S.

ATHENA PRESS
LONDON

ISBN 10-digit: 1 84748 190 6
ISBN 13-digit: 978 1 84748 190 0

First Published 2008 by
ATHENA PRESS
Queen's House, 2 Holly Road
Twickenham TW1 4EG
United Kingdom

Please note that the use of prayers attributed
to Medugorje in no way prejudices
any statement from the Vatican on the
authenticity of the apparitions.

Imprimatur and Nihil Obstat
Cum permissu superiorum
John Gilmartin VG
Glasgow, 22 May 2007

Printed for Athena Press

This book is dedicated
to
the Most Holy Trinity
and to
Mary Mother of God,
Queen of Peace.

I wish most sincerely to thank my sponsors,
Mr Kevin & Mrs Catherine McPhilomy,
for their generous support and encouragement.
This book is most respectfully devoted
to the memory of their beloved daughter,
Clare Ann McPhilomy.

The drawings are courtesy of the distinguished artist,
John August Swanson.

My grateful thanks go to Miss Angela Ferrier
for typing the manuscript.

Contents

Foreword

he Virgin Mary lived a seemingly ordinary life in Nazareth. She loved God in and through the very normality of everyday living, for she was engaged in the small things of life in humble simplicity.

Mary was receptive of the angel's message to her for she was simple and pure in soul, and welcomed God's choice of her in love and through love.

It is in the familiar routines of our daily lives that God speaks to us.

If we ourselves live long enough we shall grow old but, looking back on our lives, we will nevertheless judge them to have been very short.

From God's plan for the whole of creation as set down in the opening chapters of Genesis, we can deduce that God has also a definite plan for each one of us.

God gave us understanding, willpower, affectivity, freedom to serve.

Each day is God's gift to us, a gift of love that leads to an appreciation that all is gift, given to us in love. God's greatest gift to us is the capacity to love – to give and receive love, love that enlarges other people through the small daily little unremembered acts of kindness and love, love that uplifts and makes people feel significant, important, as having a dignity that lifts their lives to a higher level of purposefulness.

We are privileged to have the gift of giving. Sometimes we betray that love in anger, resentment, unkind words. But love makes all things new and is purified in sacrifice and tears.

The years that remain to us are gifts from God to learn how love is all-forgiving, all-healing, all-understanding, all-thankful and humbly grateful.

Mary, as the messenger of God's love, is our guide and companion, and mother on our life's way.

The rosary takes us in contemplative prayer through all the events in the life of her divine Son, and does so in a peaceful, calm, uplifting rhythm, as we walk in love on the path that Jesus trod.

Through his sufferings, death and resurrection, Jesus gives Himself to us in the Eucharist, the living Bread of life.

May Mary, the Mother of the Eucharist, be with us in our prayerful observance of her feasts throughout the liturgical year.

1 January

Solemnity of Mary, Mother of God

Hail holy Mother! The child to whom you gave birth is the King of heaven and earth.

Sedulius, ninth century

We revere the Blessed Virgin as the Mother of God, the ever-pure virgin woman, the perfect mother, and one who knows the depths of human suffering, having borne witness to the agonizing and humiliating death of her divine Son.

Oxford Companion to the Bible

Our veneration and love of the Blessed Virgin Mary is founded on the gospels and the living tradition that enriches them. There are several types of the Blessed Virgin Mary in the Old Testament: Eve, the mother of all the living; Noah's ark, wherein the human race was saved from extinction, and the Ark of the Covenant, containing manna and the tablets of the law. This Ark was the focus of God's presence as the Israelites made their way through the wilderness. Then there is Judith who slew Holofernes, the arch enemy of her people; Esther who was exempted from the universal law forbidding access to the king, without his permission, and by her mediation saved her people from death. The mother of the seven Maccabees who encouraged her sons to endure death as martyrs to the Law of God. But Mary, our Mother, is absolutely unique for she is the Mother of eternal Son of God made man, who is God Himself. In the Book of the Revelation, we read:

Now a great sign appeared in heaven: a woman adorned with the sun, standing on the moon, with twelve stars on her head for a crown.

The woman brought a male child into the world, the son who was to rule all the nations with an iron sceptre, and the child was taken straight up to God and His throne, while the woman escaped into the desert, where God made a place of safety ready.

Revelations 12:1–6[*]

Then the dragon was enraged with the woman and went away to make war on the rest of her children, that is, all who obey God's commandments and bear witness for Jesus.

Revelations 12:17

We turn to Jesus our Redeemer and to Mary our Mother for protection against the evil one. The evil one will molest no one who is wearing a crucifix or religious medal round the neck.

In her lifetime, Mary had great honour paid to her: the angel Gabriel addressed her as '...so highly favoured; [full of grace] Mary do not be afraid, you have won God's favour.' (Luke 1:43)

Elizabeth was the first to call her 'Mother of God': 'Why should I be honoured with a visit from the mother of my Lord? (Luke 1:43).

Mary, inspired by the Holy Spirit, replied:

My soul glorifies the Lord, my spirit rejoices in God my Saviour. He looks upon His servant in her lowliness; henceforth all generations will call me blessed.

Luke 1:28

Our simple, traditional Christmas carols contain truths of great depth, and entice us, as it were, to come into the stable at Bethlehem in humble adoration:

> The snow lay on the ground, the stars shone bright,
> When Christ our Lord was born on Christmas night.
> Twas Mary daughter pure of holy Anne
> That brought into this world our God made Man.

---

[*] All biblical quotes are taken from the Jerusalem Bible

She laid him in a stall at Bethlehem;
The ass and oxen shared the roof with them.
St Joseph too was by to tend the Child
To guard Him and protect His mother mild.
The angels hovered round and sang this song:
Venite adoremus Dominum,
Venite adoremus Dominum.
And thus that manger poor became a throne;
For He Whom Mary bore was God the Son.
O come, then let us join the heavenly host,
To praise the father, Son and Holy Ghost.
Venite adoremus Dominum,
Venite adoremus Dominum.

The Angelus salutation, morning, noon and evening, and also the rosary, call to mind that it is through the obedience of Mary that the human race is restored to God's favour and grace. Through one woman, Eve, came death: through Mary, the new Eve, came everlasting life.

I loved her more than health or beauty, preferred her to the light since her radiance never sleeps. In her company all good things came to me, at her hands riches not to be numbered.

Wisdom 7:10–11

Who can doubt that the Son will listen to His mother – such a Son to such a mother!

St Bernard of Clairvaux, 1090–1153

What honours He has conferred upon her – He who commanded us to honour our parents.

St John Damascene, 676–749

Today, on the Feast of the Solemnity of the Mother of God, let us first thank Jesus, her divine Son, for being for us 'the bread of Life' as our daily spiritual food.

It is Mary, our Mother, who has made possible this heavenly food. Let us thank our Blessed Lady for her most loving care for us. In a very special way this Feast for us is 'Mother's Day'. So let us show our loving appreciation for all that our mothers and fathers have done for us. It would be great comfort to them if we were to say today: 'Mum, I love you!', 'Dad, I love you!' They have worked hard to give us a good life. Our mother has made many sacrifices to provide a happy home while our father has worked very hard in the industrial and commercial world to provide our daily bread and all that we reasonably need. On this holy day let us thank Almighty God for the gift of this beautiful universe and for all the living creatures on land, sea and air. They are beautiful sinless beings and God has appointed us to respect and care for them. We are the stewards of creation. God blessed Adam and Eve, saying,

> Be fruitful, fill the earth and conquer it. Be masters of the fish of the sea, the birds of heaven and all living animals on the earth!

> Genesis 1:28

> God saw all that He had made, and indeed it was very good!

> Genesis 1:31

In the quiet days of their family life in Nazareth, Mary was a worthy housewife. She fetched water from the village well, swept the floor, washed clothes, baked bread, and cooked wholesome meals. She would feed the neighbouring children who came to her door with choice titbits, as well as providing food for beggars and passing wayfarers. She would visit her sick neighbours, listen to their stories and comfort them. They would admire her gentle cheerfulness and her love for everyone. Our Blessed Mother was an excellent seamstress and made clothing for Jesus and St Joseph. The soldiers on Calvary paid unwitting tribute to her skill. When the soldiers had finished crucifying Jesus they took his clothing and divided it into four shares, one for each soldier. His under-garment was seamless, woven in one piece from neck to hem; so they said to one another, 'Let us throw dice to decide who is to have it.' (John 19:23–24) The soldiers could see that the garment was a work of art.

Jesus, Mary and Joseph would pray together and perhaps,

from time to time, would chant and sing one of the psalms of King David:

> Let us sing a new song to the Lord, for the Lord takes delight in his people, and crowns the poor with salvation.
>   Let the faithful rejoice in their glory, shout for joy and take their rest.

Psalm 149:1, 4–5

We have fond memories of our school days when the May altar was festooned with candles, flowers, a winsome statue of our Lady and robust singing of Marial hymns:

> Hail Queen of heaven, the ocean star! Guide of the wanderer here below!

All the saints without exception had a great devotion to the holy Mother of God and followed her example in the service of God and his people.

Daily Prayer of the Divine Office

Evening Prayer 1

Antiphon 3

> Moses saw the thorn bush which was on fire yet was not burnt up. In it we see a sign of your virginity which all must honour: Mother of God pray for us.

Morning Prayer

Antiphon 3

> Mary gave birth to the king whose name is eternal; she united the joy of a mother with the honour of a

virgin; such as this has never happened before nor will it happen again, alleluia!

Benedictus Antiphon

Today a wonderful mystery is announced, something new has taken place: God has become man. He remained what he was and has become that which he was not, and though the two natures remain distinct, he is one.

Intercessions

Lord Jesus, may your gift of faith grow stronger in us every day – and find expression in our ways of living.

Evening Prayer 2

Antiphon 1

O wonderful exchange! The creator of human nature took on a human body and was born of the Virgin. He became man without having a human father and has bestowed on us his divine nature.

Intercessions:

You gave the Virgin Mary the joys of motherhood – grant to all parents joy in their children. Son of the Virgin Mary hear our prayer. You were born into a human family – strengthen with love the bonds of family life. Son of the Virgin Mary, hear our prayer.

Concluding Prayer

God, our Father, since you have given mankind a saviour through Blessed Mary, Virgin and Mother, grant that we may feel the power of her intercession when she pleads for us with Jesus Christ, your Son, the author of life, who lives and reigns with you and the Holy Spirit, God, for ever and ever. Amen.

Dear children!
Today I call you to open yourselves to prayer. May prayer become joy for you. Renew prayer in your families and form prayer groups. In this way, you will experience joy in prayer and togetherness. All those who pray and are members of prayer groups are open to God's will in their hearts and joyfully witness to God's love. I am with you, I carry all of you in my heart and I bless you with my motherly blessing. Thank you for having responded to my call.

Our Lady of Peace, Medugorje, September, 2000

2 FEBRUARY

THE PRESENTATION OF THE LORD

t is important to reflect on the reason why we celebrate feasts and festivals. From the beginning of time human beings have celebrated feasts and virtually all of them were religious in origin and character.

> When Noah came out of the Ark with his family and animals he built an altar for Yahweh, God, and choosing from the clean animals and all the clean birds, he offered burnt offerings on the altar.

> Genesis 8:20

He did so in thanksgiving that the world had been saved from extinction. Our ancestors had various rituals for expressing their desire to rejoice in the blessings of life and nature; sometimes offering sacrifice with burnt offerings. This was their way of uniting the world with the divine and through passing on their religious traditions to their offspring, endeavoured to bond their society in a communal ethos. These were family or group celebrations marking the change of season, the New Year, births and other notable events. They deemed these communal events worthy of celebration: no joy was complete for them unless it could be shared. To receive the spiritual riches of the various liturgical feasts we must appropriate them and engage with them in the prayer of the universal Church, which is the holy sacrifice of the Mass, '...the fountain of all holiness'.

> The law of prayer is the law of faith: the Church believes as she prays.

> Prosper of Aquitaine, fifth century

If Christians have celebrated the Eucharist from the beginning and in a form whose substance has not changed despite the great diversity of times and liturgies, it is because we know ourselves to be bound by the command the Lord gave on the eve of His Passion: 'Do this in remembrance of me'.

1 Corinthians 11:24–25,
Catechism of the Catholic Church, no. 1356

It is in the spirit of this living tradition that we celebrate the feasts of the Blessed Virgin Mary, the holy Mother of God.

Cry out with joy to the Lord all the earth; serve the Lord with gladness.

Psalm 47:1

The priest celebrant welcomes the people in these words:

'Forty days ago we celebrated the joyful feast of the birth of our Lord Jesus Christ. Today we recall the holy day on which He was presented in the temple, fulfilling the Law of Moses and at the same time going to meet his faithful people. Led by the Spirit, Simeon and Anna came to the temple, recognised Christ as their Lord, and proclaimed Him with joy.'

The celebration of today's feast is one of the most ancient in the Church. It recapitulates the central event of the Old Testament, the Exodus, the escape of the Hebrews from slavery in Egypt in the thirteenth century BC. The theme of struggle to be free from slavery is enacted through all subsequent history. At the moment of the Transfiguration, St Luke describes Jesus' passion, death and resurrection as an Exodus, a passing, a departure:

Suddenly there were two men there talking to Him; they were Moses and Elijah appearing in glory, and they were speaking of his passing which He was to accomplish in Jerusalem.

Luke 9:3–31

In order to commemorate the Exodus in perpetuity as an act of thanksgiving, Moses decreed:

> Consecrate all the first-born to me, the first issue of every womb among the sons of Israel. Whether man or beast, this is mine.

> Exodus 13:2

Accordingly, forty days after the new birth, the child must be brought to the Temple and redeemed by an offering of two turtle doves and the mother, purified by making a similar offering. It had been revealed to Simeon by the holy Spirit that he would not see death until he had set eyes on the Christ (the anointed One) of the Lord. Prompted by the Spirit, he came into the Temple and when the parents brought the child in to do that the Law required, he took Him in his arms and blessed God; and he said:

> Now Master, you can let your servant go in peace, just as you promised; because my eyes have seen the salvation which you have prepared for all nations to see, a light to enlighten the pagans, and the glory of your people, Israel.

> Luke 2:27–32

Simeon blessed Mary and Joseph and said to Mary his mother,

> You see this child; he is destined for the fall and the rising of many in Israel, destined to a be a sign that is rejected – and a sword will pierce your own soul too – so that the secret thoughts of many may be laid bare.

> Luke 2:34–35

The prophetess, Anna, shared Simeon's joy at the revelation of the salvation, '…prepared for all the nations to see.' (Luke 2:38)

The prophecy of Simeon brought home to his parents that the mission of Jesus would not only entail suffering for the Saviour of the world but also for His mother, Mary, who was the very first to offer up Jesus as a victim for our redemption. The Father, to reward her generosity, made her, through Christ, the dispenser of the riches and graces of God. Jesus in Mary's arms is a reminder that redemption can only come through her son Jesus.

Later:

The everyday obedience of Jesus to his mother and legal father fulfils the fourth commandment perfectly and was the temporal image of his filial obedience to his Father in Heaven. The everyday obedience of Jesus to Mary and Joseph both announced and anticipated the obedience of Holy Thursday: 'Not my will, but thine be done.' The obedience of Christ in the daily routine of his hidden life was already inaugurating his work of restoring what the disobedience of Adam had destroyed.

Catechism of the Catholic Church, no. 532

The Son of Man came not to be served but to serve and to give his life as a ransom for many.

Matthew 20:28

The Presentation in the Temple marks the very beginning of Jesus' vocation to redeem humankind by His life, death and resurrection.

As by one man's disobedience many were made sinners, so by one man's obedience many will be made righteous.

Romans 5:19

This feast of today invites us to look ahead to the childhood years of Jesus: the finding of Jesus in the temple is the only event that breaks the silence of the gospels about His hidden years. Here Jesus lets us catch a glimpse of the mystery of His total consecration to a mission that flows from His divine Sonship.

Did you not know that I must be about my Father's work?

Luke 2:41–52

Mary and Joseph did not understand these words, but they accepted them in faith. Mary kept all these things in her heart during the years Jesus remained hidden in the silence of an ordinary life.

Catechism of the Catholic Church no 534

During the greater part of His life Jesus shared the condition of the vast majority of human beings: a daily life without evident greatness, a life of manual labour. His religious life was that of a Jew obedient to the Law of God – a life in the community.

Catechism of the Catholic Church, no. 531

When the appointed time came, God sent His Son, born of a woman born a subject of the Law, to redeem the subjects of the Law and to enable us to be adopted as sons.

Galatians 4:4

The hidden life of Jesus in Nazareth allows everyone to enter into fellowship with Jesus in the most ordinary events of family life; the home of Nazareth is the school of the gospel. First then, a lesson of silence. May esteem for silence, that admirable and indispensable condition of mind, be renewed in us – a lesson of family life. May Nazareth teach us what family life is. Its communion of love, its sincere and simple beauty, its sacred and inviolable character – a lesson of work. Nazareth, home of the Carpenter's Son, you I would choose to understand and proclaim the severe and redeeming law of human work.

Catechism of the Catholic Church, no. 533. Pope Paul VI at Nazareth, 1964

This Feast of the Presentation of the Lord is also a reminder that 'the desire for God is written in the human heart because man is created by God and for God; and God never ceases to draw man to Himself. Only in God will he find the happiness and the truth he never stops searching for.

Catechism of the Catholic Church, no. 27

God created us in love:

Anyone who lives in love lives in God and God lives in him.

John 1:4–16

Your love has guided the people you redeemed: your power has led them to your holy dwelling place.

Exodus 15:17–18

So I say to you: ask, and it will be given to you; search and you will find; knock, and the door will be opened to you.

For the one who asks always receives; the one who searches always finds; the one who knocks will always have the door opened to him.

Luke 11:9–10

Let the hearts of those who seek the Lord rejoice!

Psalm 105:3

You have made us for yourself, and our heart is restless until it rests in you.

St Augustine, fifth century

In our own day, the lighting of candles has become a popular way of expressing support and sympathy for the bereaved. Also friends will say to you: 'I will light a candle for you and pray for you at such and such a shrine.' In Old Testament times, candles were unknown. Instead, small earthen lamps were used in which a wick floating in oil gave a feeble light. Scripture uses the term 'lamp':

Man's spirit is the lamp of Yahweh, searching his deepest self.

Proverbs 20:27

In the west from the second century onwards, candles were used in funeral processions, and also at the tombs of martyrs. Then candles began to be used to light up churches and from the eleventh century were placed on the altar table in honour of the resurrection of our Lord Jesus Christ.

The wax candles signify the mankind of the divine infant. The wick figures His soul and the flame of his Godhead.

St Anselm, 1033–1109

The candles upon the altar, furthermore, signify the presence of Him Who is the light of the world, the God-man, Who enlightens us by His word.

Candlemas recalls the journey of Mary and Joseph to the temple to present the Child Jesus as the Law ordained:

> Look I am going to send my messenger to prepare a way before me. And the Lord you are seeking will suddenly enter his Temple.
>
> Malachi 3:1

The Blessing of Candles

Let us pray.
God our Father, source of all light, today you revealed to Simeon your Light of revelation to the nations. Bless these candles and make them holy. May we who carry them to praise your glory walk in the path of goodness and come to the light that shines for ever.

Preface

Father, all-powerful and ever-living God, we do well always and everywhere to give you thanks through Jesus Christ our Lord. Today your Son who shares your eternal splendour was presented in the temple, and revealed by the Spirit as the glory of Israel and the light of all peoples. Our hearts are joyful, for we have seen your salvation, and now with the angels and saints we praise you for ever.

> You who wanted no sacrifice or oblation, prepared a body for me. You took no pleasure in holocausts or sacrifices for sin; then I said, just as I was commanded in the scroll of the book, 'God, here I am! I am coming to obey your will!'
>
> Hebrews 10:5–7

Dear children!
Today I call you to accept and live my messages with seriousness. These days are the days when you need to decide for God, for peace and for the good. May every hatred and jealousy disappear from your life and your thoughts, and may there only dwell love for God and for your neighbour. Thus, and only thus shall you be able to discern the signs of the time. I am with you and guide you into a new time God gives you as grace so that you may get to know Him even more. Thank you for having responded to my call.

Our Lady of Peace, Medugorje, January 1993

Holy Michael, the Archangel, defend us in the day of battle: be our safeguard against the wickedness and snares of the devil. May God rebuke him we humbly pray, and do thou Prince of the heavenly host by the power of God thrust down to hell Satan and all wicked spirits who wander through the world for the ruin of souls.

St Michael and the Archangels
Copyright © John August Swanson 2006

11 FEBRUARY

OUR LADY OF LOURDES

Fourteen-year-old Bernadette Soubirous, scrupulously clean in her threadbare clothes and wooden clogs, set out with her younger sister Toinette and her cousin Jeane Abadie, to search for firewood along the banks of the River Gave in Lourdes, in the south of France near the Spanish border. Bernadette was small for her age, had been a victim of cholera at the age of eleven and was very asthmatic. She had hardly ever been to school and could neither read nor write, and had not as yet made her first Holy Communion. While about to wade to the other side of the river, she suddenly saw a beautiful Lady in the niche of the rock of Massabielle on the other side of the water. She said later, 'I had hardly begun to take off my stocking when I heard the sound of wind as in a storm. I turned towards the meadow, and I saw that the trees were not moving at all. I had half-noticed, but without paying any particular attention, that the brambles and bushes were waving beside the grotto. I went on taking off my stockings, and was putting one foot in the water, when I heard the same sound in front of me. I looked up and saw a cluster of branches and brambles underneath the topmost opening of the grotto, tossing and swaying to and fro, though nothing stirred all around. Behind these branches and within the opening, I saw immediately a girl no bigger than myself, who greeted me with a slight bow of the head. At the same time, she stretched out her arms slightly away from her body, opening her hands as in the pictures of Our Lady. Over her right arm hung a rosary. I was afraid. I stepped back. I wanted to call the two little girls; but I hadn't the courage to do so. I rubbed my eyes again and again; I thought I must be mistaken. Raising my eyes again, I saw a girl smiling at me most graciously and seeming to invite me to come nearer. But I was still afraid. It was not however a fear such as I have had at other times, for I would have stayed there for ever looking at her; whereas when you are afraid you run away quickly. Then I thought of saying my prayers. I put my hand in my pocket. I took out my rosary which I usually carry on me. I knelt down and tried to make the sign of the cross but I could not lift my hand to my forehead; it fell back. The girl, meanwhile, stepped to one side and turned towards me. This time she was holding the large beads in her hand. She crossed herself as if to pray. My hand was trembling. I tried to make the sign of the cross, and this time I could. After that I was not afraid. I said my rosary. The young girl slipped the beads of hers through her fingers, but she was not moving her lips, but she joined in saying the 'Glory be to the Father...' While I was saying the rosary, I was watching as hard as I could. She was wearing a white dress reaching down to her feet, which meant that only her toes were visible. The dress was gathered very high at the neck by a hem from which hung a white cord. A white veil covered her head and came down over her shoulders and arms almost to the bottom of her dress. On each foot I saw a yellow rose. The sash of the dress was blue and hung down below her knees. The chain of the rosary was yellow; the beads white and widely spaced. The girl was alive, very young, and surrounded with a soft bright light. When I finished my rosary, she bowed to me smiling. She retired within the niche and disappeared all of a sudden.'

Though Bernadette's family were extremely poor, the parents had such a noble character that they would never accept presents or gifts of money from anyone at any time. Their faith in God was simple but very strong, sustained by daily family prayer and devotions, and their deep love for one another and their children. Bernadette suffered from chronic ill health but never complained. She brought great consolation to the family and was loved by them very much. Forbidden to go to the grotto because of the crowds that her apparitions had drawn, Bernadette could only reply, 'I feel myself drawn by an irresistible force.'

Bernadette never wished to speak about the apparitions: she wanted to remain hidden and out of the way. She suffered a great deal from the demands of people wanting to know all about her experience.

The Blessed Virgin appeared to Bernadette eighteen times and told her that she would die young, 'I do not promise to make you happy in this world, but in the next.'

'When you have seen her once, you would willingly die to see her again,' Bernadette said.

The Lady asked for prayers and penance for the conversion of sinners and told Bernadette she wished people to come in procession and bring their sick children with them. She also asked for a chapel to be built there. At the ninth apparition, the Lady said to Bernadette, 'Go and drink at the spring and wash yourself in it!' Bernadette could only see a trickle of muddy water, but she sipped a little and in the process dirtied her face at which some of the unbelieving crowd jeered at her.

Since that time, however, the 'spring' has never ceased to flow copiously and millions of pilgrims have been pleased to bring home some Lourdes water. Towards the end of the series of apparitions several miraculous cures took place.

One was of a child suffering from paralysis of the spine. A doctor was present and persuaded the parents to undress the child and hold him under the flow of the 'spring' which they did for about six minutes. They then dried the boy and laid him on the ground but he immediately got up and ran to his father and mother, who hugged him and covered him with kisses, shedding tears of joy all the while.

On the 1 March 1858, a young priest, Abbé Dezirat, had come to Lourdes to see for himself what was taking place at the grotto. He fixed his eyes on Bernadette in ecstasy. 'By her posture and by the expression of her face, it was evident that her soul was enraptured. What profound peace! What serenity! What lofty contemplation! Her smile was beyond all description. The child's gaze, fixed on the apparition, was no less captivating. Impossible to imagine anything so pure, so sweet, so loving. Oh, how good it was to be there! I felt my self on the threshold of paradise!' The awed silence of the crowds when Bernadette was in ecstasy made a profound impression on everyone present at the grotto. 'We would like to have stayed there for ever,' one commented.

The local parish priest had been insisting that Bernadette ask the lady her name. Bernadette had done so several times, but on the Feast of Annunciation, 25 March 1858, Bernadette asked, 'Madame, will you be so kind as to tell me who you are?'

Raising her eyes to heaven, the lady replied, 'I am the Immaculate Conception.' The lady smiled, spoke no more and disappeared, still smiling.

Little Bernadette had no idea what these words meant and kept repeating them to herself so as to be able to convey these words to the parish priest.

Four years previously on 8 December 1854, Pope Pius IX proclaimed what most Catholics had always believed – that the Blessed Virgin from the first moment of her conception was preserved from all stain of original sin through the merits of her divine Son. This statement of the Blessed Virgin confirmed the veracity of all that Bernadette had experienced in the Apparitions at Massabielle.

During the seventeenth apparition the local medic, Doctor Duzous, held a lighted candle under Bernadette's hand, but she felt nothing. The final apparition took place on Friday, 16 July 1858, and lasted fifteen minutes. 'Never had I seen Bernadette looking so beautiful,' said one witness. At one time, upon being asked what the lady's smile was like, Bernadette replied, 'Oh, sir, you would have to come from heaven itself to reproduce that smile. Once you have seen her you never have any more liking for this earth.'

Bernadette's own features and clear gaze were like a mirror reflecting the purity and innocence of her soul. Bernadette was sixteen-and-a-half years old by now and was suffering constantly from the pains of rheumatism, was vomiting blood and having heart palpitations and violent attacks of asthma. She never complained and offered up her suffering for the conversion of sinners. Despite this, there were still many people wanting to question her about the apparitions and this was very fatiguing for her.

Ultimately, Bernadette entered the order of the Sisters of Notre Dame de Nevers. In due course she was given the task of assistant infirmarian and treated the sick with great affection and was loved by them. She had also developed into an excellent seamstress and became a graceful script writer.

It was natural that the sisters wished to protect Bernadette from becoming vain and proud because of her intimacy with the Blessed Virgin.

In this way Bernadette was subject to not a few humiliations. The sister who was secretary of the annals of the novitiate recorded that Bernadette was '…humble in her supernatural triumph, simple and unassuming, even though everything so far conspired to exalt her and advertise.' Adding to all Bernadette's suffering was the coldness of the Mother Provincial, who on one occasion said, 'I don't understand why the Blessed Virgin appeared to Bernadette. There are so many others so refined, so well-bred.' Bernadette compared herself to a sweeping brush which after it is used is put behind the door. She said, 'The Blessed Virgin used me and then put me back in my place. The Blessed Virgin chose me because she could not find anyone more stupid than I am!'

She had confided to her notebook, 'For love of Jesus I will carry the cross hidden in my heart.'

When she was near death she begged the Mother Superior's forgiveness for all her failures in the religious life (infidelities). Her dying words were, 'Holy Mary, Mother of God, pray for me… poor sinner… poor sinner… poor sinner…'

St Bernadette's beautiful incorrupt body rests in the chapel of the Convent of Nevers for all to see and venerate.

All of us can take great encouragement from the life of St Bernadette. As one so highly favoured by God through His Blessed Mother, the Virgin Mary, it is very important to note that St Bernadette suffered a very great deal all her life from the pains of rheumatism, asthma, violent vomiting, palpitations and physical weakness.

Never in her thirty-five years of life did she enjoy good robust health. Her family were extremely poor and were housed in what can only be described as an airless dungeon. But father, mother, younger sisters and brothers were united in a close bond of love and so were a deeply happy family.

Bernadette was a very loving, humble person who desired to

be unnoticed and forgotten. She was possessed by a great peace for her love was nurtured by constant prayer, especially the rosary. She was truly beautiful in the beauty of holiness. In the convent when she was assistant infirmarian she was much loved by all those who came under her gentle care.

Love is the most beautiful gift we can give to anyone, especially anyone who is suffering. Let us ask St Bernadette to help us walk closer to God in prayer, penance, uprightness, love.

> The bells of the Angelus
> Calleth to pray,
> in sweet tones announcing
> The sacred Ave.
>
> Ave, Ave, Ave Maria
> Ave, Ave, Ave Maria
>
> And angel of mercy
> Led Bernadette's feet
> Where flows the deep torrent –
> Our Lady to greet
>
> Ave, Ave, Ave Maria
> Ave, Ave, Ave Maria
>
> Then rose on a sudden
> A wind strong and wild,
> The hour of grace coming
> Made known to the child
>
> Ave, Ave, Ave Maria
> Ave, Ave, Ave Maria
>
> On Massabielle
> With wondering eyes
> She saw in her glory
> The morning star rise.

Ave, Ave, Ave Maria
Ave, Ave, Ave Maria

Traditional hymn sung to a French peasant tune

19 March

Solemnity of St Joseph

S t Joseph had made up his mind to informally divorce Mary, his wife, but the angel of the Lord appeared to him in a dream and said,

> Joseph, son of David, do not be afraid to take Mary home as your wife, because she has conceived what is in her by the Holy Spirit. She is to give birth to a son and you must name him 'Jesus', because he is the one to save the people from their sins.

> Matthew 1:20–21

Now, this took place to fulfil the words spoken by the Lord through the prophet,

> The maiden is with child and will soon give birth to a son whom she will call Immanuel.

> Isaiah 7:14

The name means, 'God is with us.' (Matthew 1:19–24)

St Joseph must have been distressed when no one could be found to give them shelter in Bethlehem, for Mary's time had come and so the Lord of heaven and earth was born in a stable and laid in a manger. After the Magi had left the angel of the lord appeared in a dream and said,

> Get up, take the child and his mother with you, and escape into Egypt and stay there until I tell you, because Herod intends to search for the child and do away with him.

> Matthew 2:13

After Herod's death, the angel of the Lord appeared in a dream to Joseph in Egypt and said,

> Get up, and take the child and his mother with you and go back to the land of Israel, for those who wanted to kill the child are dead.

Matthew 2:20

Bethlehem and Nazareth, places favoured by God's providence, were the meeting place between the plans of the emperor and the will of God. Through angelic visitations St Joseph was privy to heavenly secrets and was charged with the guidance and support, well-being and safety of both Mary and her Child. St Joseph was indeed a very special friend of God. Jesus, though divine, loved to call Himself 'Son of man'. St Joseph was granted the honour for which kings and prophets sighed,

> Joseph might take the Child in his arms, kiss him, speak to Him, and protect Him.

St Bernard, twelfth century

> He was called 'Father' by Him whose Father was in heaven.

St Basil, fourth century

Joseph was '...that faithful and wise servant whom the Lord has set over His household.' (Matthew 25:23)

The Virgin Mother was surely disquieted by the enigmatic prophecy of the aged Simeon in the Temple:

> You see this Child; He is destined to be a sign that is rejected – and a sword will pierce your own soul too, that the thoughts of many may be laid bare.

Luke 2:35

St Joseph, a just and honourable man, would have supported and comforted her in her fears:

My God, make your ways known to me teach me your paths. Set me on the way of your truth, and teach me, for you are the God who saves me.

Psalm 25:3–5

For me the reward of virtue is to see your face, and on waking to gaze my fill on your likeness.

Psalm 7:15

The Mother of Jesus regarded Joseph as having equal parental rights. He would have shared Mary's grief at the loss of their twelve-year-old child: 'Your father and I have sought you sorrowing.' (Luke 24:8) But the meaning of this mystery is hidden from them:

He went down with them and came to Nazareth and lived under their authority. His Mother stored all these things in her heart. And Jesus increased in wisdom, in stature and favour with God and men.

Luke 2:51–52

In later years the people of his home town were unwilling to accept Him:

What is this wisdom that has been granted Him, and these miracles that are worked through Him? This is the carpenter surely, the Son of Mary? And they would not accept Him.

Mark 6:2–4

Jesus learned his carpentry from St Joseph as well as assuming his manner of speech and that of His Mother. St Joseph, husband of Mary, was foreshadowed in the Old Testament by Joseph who was sold into slavery in Egypt by his brothers. But God's hand was with him. He was made vice-regent in the court of Pharaoh and who, to mark his confidence in Joseph, '…took the ring from his hand and put it on Joseph's.' (Genesis 41:55)

When Egypt began to suffer from famine, Pharaoh told his people, 'Go to Joseph and do what he tells you!' (Genesis 41:55)

Joseph saved the people of his time from famine. St Joseph was the saviour and guardian of the two most important persons in the whole world, the Child Jesus, and His Mother, Mary.

> A faithful man shall be greatly praised; and he that is the keeper of the Lord shall be glorified.
>
> Proverbs 2:7

> The Lord loved him and adorned him; He clothed him with a robe of glory.
>
> Ecclesiasticus 45:9

St Joseph was close to the fountain of all holiness all his life, just as the spring is clearer as we approach the source. He is therefore considered the patron and model of the interior and contemplative life.

We pray to St Joseph for the grace of a holy and a happy death, for Jesus and His Mother were by his side in his last moments and he died in their arms. Pius IX in 1870 was pleased to declare that St Joseph was to be regarded as the Protector and Guardian of the universal Church.

All the great saints were named as servants of God: Joseph alone was dignified by the title of 'Father'. By his familiar conversations with Jesus and Mary he absorbed something of the divine mysteries. He had the complete confidence of Jesus and Mary. Neither St Matthew nor St Luke have recorded any words of St Joseph, unassuming in his simplicity. His quiet personality makes him a very likeable saint.

Preface from the Mass in Honour of St Joseph

> Father, all-powerful and ever-living God, we do well always and everywhere to give you thanks, as we honour St Joseph. He is that just man, the wise and loyal servant, whom you placed at the head of your family. With a husband's love he cherished Mary, the Virgin Mother of God. With

fatherly affection he watched over Jesus Christ, your Son, conceived by the power of the Holy Spirit.

Through Christ the choirs of angels and all the powers of heaven praise and worship your glory. May our voices blend with theirs as we join in their unending hymn: Holy, holy, holy...

Prayer to St Joseph (Pope Leo XIII)

To you, O blessed Joseph, we have recourse in our tribulations, and while imploring the aid of your most holy spouse, we invoke your patronage also. By that love which united you to the Immaculate Virgin, Mother of God. And by the fatherly affection with which you embraced the infant, Jesus, we humbly beseech you graciously to regard the inheritance which Jesus purchased by His blood, and help us in our necessities by your powerful intercession.

Protect, O most provident guardian of the Holy family the chosen people of Jesus Christ; ward off from us all taint of error and corruption. Graciously assist us from heaven, O most powerful Protector in our struggle with the powers of darkness, and as you did once rescue the Child Jesus from imminent peril to His life, so now defend the Holy Church from the snares of her enemies and from all adversity. Shield each one of us with your unceasing patronage, that, imitating your example, and supported by your aid, we may be enabled to live a good life, die a happy death, and secure everlasting happiness in heaven.

Amen.

Morning Prayer from the Divine Office

Intercessions

1. Joseph took the Child Jesus into his care, loving and accepting Him as his own Son. May we accept all that God gives us, and care for those entrusted to us.

2. As Joseph believed what you had told him, and became the guardian of Your only Son, so may we put our faith in you, and receive the fulfilment of your promise.

Evening Prayer

Father, you enabled Joseph to spend his life in your service. Set our minds on your kingdom and your justice before all other things. Creator of all things, you have entrusted your work to our hands. Grant that our labours may prove worthy of you.

Father, hallowed be your name.

Hymn

Dear St Joseph, pure and gentle,
Guardian of the Saviour Child
Treading with the Virgin Mother
Egypt's deserts rough and wild.

Chorus:
Hail St Joseph, spouse of Mary,
Blessed above all saints on high,
When the death shades round us gather
Teach oh teach us how to die.

He who rested on thy bosom
Is by countless saints adored;
Prostrate angels in his presence
Sing hosannas to their Lord.

Now to thee no gift refusing
Jesus stoops to hear thy prayer
Then dear saint from thy fair dwelling
Give to us father's care.

Dear St Joseph, kind and loving,
Stretch to us a helping hand,
Guide us through life's toils and sorrows
Safely to the distant land.

Dear children!
Also today, I call you to open yourselves to prayer.
Especially now in this time of grace, open your
hearts, little children, and express your love to the
Crucified. Only in this way, will you discover peace,
and prayer will begin to flow from your heart into
the world. Be an example, little children, and an
incentive for good. I am close to you and I love you
all. Thank you for having responded to my call.

Our Lady of Peace, Medugorje, 25 March 2004

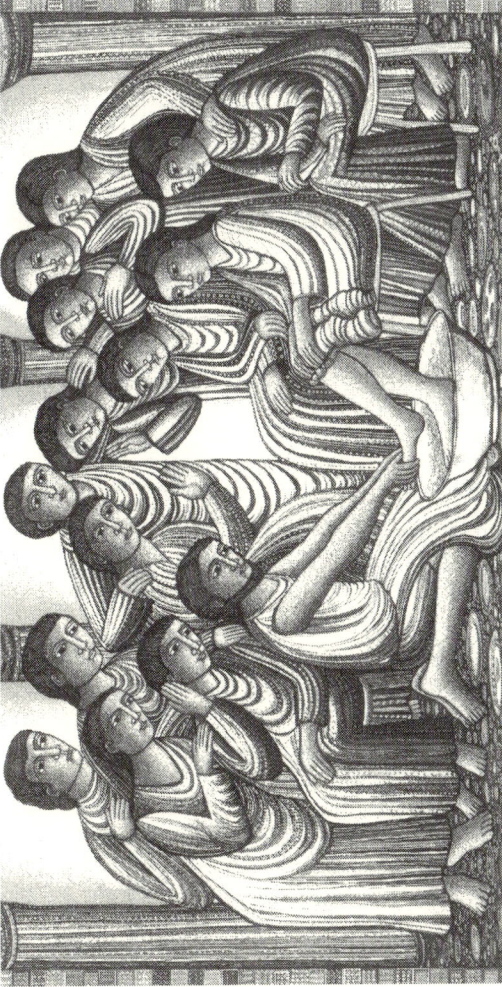

Washing of the Feet
Copyright © John August Swanson 2000

25 MARCH

SOLEMNITY OF THE ANNUNCIATION

As Christ came into the world, he said: Behold! I have come to do your will, O God.

Hebrews 10:76–7

The Angel Gabriel was sent to the prophet, Daniel, to enlighten him as to the time when Christ would be born, and to Zechariah, at the hour in which he offered incense in the Holy of Holies in the Temple, to announce to him the birth of John the Baptist, the herald of the Messiah.

Your wife, Elizabeth is to bear you a son and you must name him, John. Even from his mother's womb he will be filled with the Holy Spirit.

Luke 1:13–16

Only Gabriel, a name which means 'power of God' was found worthy among all the choirs of angels to announce to Mary the designs of God with regard to her.

St Bernard, twelfth century

He was chosen from all the hosts of angels to proclaim the mystery of the Incarnation. With a feeling of holy reverence, the Angel Gabriel came to the Virgin, who from all eternity had been chosen to be the Mother on earth of Him of whom God is the Father in heaven. In words inspired by the Holy Spirit, the Angel said to her: 'Hail, full of grace, the Lord is with thee: blessed art thou among women.' (Luke 1:28–38)

Seeing that Mary was taken aback by this salutation, the Angel explained that he had come to obtain her consent – her fiat – that the great mystery might be accomplished on which depended the redemption of mankind. It was Mary's wish to remain a virgin and the Angel of the Lord announced that she would conceive of the Holy Spirit and that she would give birth to a Son to whom she would give the name, Jesus, that is to say, Saviour. Then, without hesitating, Mary submitted with the most profound humility:

> Behold, the handmaid of the Lord: be it done to me according to your word.
>
> Luke 1:38

> The maiden is with child and will soon give birth to a son whom she will call Immanuel. On curds and honey will he feed until he knows how to refuse evil and choose good.
>
> Isaiah 7:14

In that instant was accomplished the greatest of all miracles when God raised to Himself and into union with Him the blessed fruit of the womb of the Virgin: 'And the Word was made flesh and dwelt among us.' (John 1:14)

The Word took upon Him our humanity, our poverty, our nothingness and gave us in return His divinity. God who made man becomes Man and enters into human history.

> You took no pleasure in holocaust or sacrifices for sin; then I said, just as I was commanded in the scroll of the book, 'God here I am! I am coming to do your will!'
>
> Hebrews 10:6–70

On this day the Word was made flesh and united to Himself for ever the humanity of Jesus.

> When the appointed time came, God sent His Son, born of a woman, a subject of the Law to redeem the subjects of the Law and to enable us to be adopted as sons.
>
> Galatians 4:4

The Word became flesh and dwelt among us, and we saw his glory, the glory that is his as the only Son of the Father, full of grace and truth.

John 1:14

It was fitting that the Mother of Him in whose body lies the fullness of divinity should herself be full of grace. In thanksgiving Mary prophesised:

My soul proclaims the greatness of the Lord, and my spirit exults in God my saviour; because he has looked upon his lowly hand-maid. Yes, from henceforth all generations will call me blessed, for the Almighty has done great things for me.

Luke 1:46–49

The Annunciation is also the anniversary of the ordination of Christ as priest, for it is by the anointing of the divinity that He has become Pontiff, Mediator between God and men. The mystery of the Incarnation has earned for Mary her most glorious title, that of 'Mother of God' (*Theotokos*).

The Son of the Father and the Son of the Virgin naturally became singular and identical Son.

St Anselm 1033–1109

At the end of the mission of the Holy Spirit, Mary became the Woman, the New Eve, Mother of all the Living, Mother of the whole Christ. Hence, Mary is Queen of the whole human race and worthy of all veneration.

Dom Gaspar Lefebrve, OSB Missal 1927

Nine months later – 25 December – is the day on which the miracle as yet known only to heaven and to the humble Virgin will be manifested to the world. The Incarnation is ascribed in a special manner to the Holy Spirit because it is the greatest work of God's love. It is interesting to note that the ancient Greeks looked to otherworldly time and space and to superhuman beings and gods to come down and mix and live with human beings.

In the month of March after the bareness of winter there are intimations of new life in trees, bushes and hedgerows. A new creative force is abroad that calls to mind the very beginning of things:

> In the beginning God created the heavens and the earth and God's spirit hovered over the waters.
>
> Genesis 1:1

The Spirit of God created light, vegetation, fish, birds, animals.

> God saw all that He had made and indeed it was very good.
>
> Genesis 1:31

The Feast of the Annunciation always takes place in March and brings an element of joy into the penitential season of Lent. In this way, we prepare through prayer and penance to greet the Risen Christ, Saviour of the World, who for ever manifests the mercy of God.

> The almighty took the form of a slave that the slave might become King.
>
> St Ambrose, fifth century

> Oh! What a wondrous redemption is that where man is, so to speak, put on a par with God.
>
> St Hilary of Poitiers, fourth century

Let the celebration of the Annunciation lead us to prayer of praise and thanksgiving, which is the holy Eucharist, '...the source and summit of all Christian life.' God makes Himself known to prayerful persons in many hidden ways. Nothing in this life can take away their inner peace and assurance for the Father, Son and Holy Spirit make their home in the soul that prays always and everywhere and in every circumstance. It is the habit of personal prayerfulness that renders our public communal prayers sincere, meaningful, and fruitful. Prayer also reveals one of the great truths of human experience, namely that 'The Kingdom of God is within you!' (Luke 7:20). Prayer, the language of love, is the breath of the soul and brings us, wherever we are, into the presence of God.

The Samaritan outcast and foreigner was the only one of the ten who came back to thank Jesus for his cleansing: 'Were not all ten made clean? The other nine, where are they?' (Luke 17:18–19)

Jesus Himself on diverse occasions gave thanks to the Father most notably:

at the multiplication of the loaves;

when He was transfigured on the mountain;

when He raised Lazarus from the dead;

at the Last Supper;

as well as at various other times.

He told his disciples:

> 'Yet do not rejoice that the spirits submit to you: rejoice rather that your names are written in heaven.' It was then that, filled with the joy in the Holy Spirit, he said, 'I Bless you Father, Lord of heaven and earth, for hiding these things from the learned and the clever and revealing them to mere children.'

> Luke 10:20–21

> My soul give thanks to the Lord and never forget his blessings.

> Psalm 103:2

We pray at holy Mass:

> Glory to God in the highest,
> And peace to his people on earth.
> Lord God, heavenly King
> Almighty God and Father,
> We worship you,
> We give you thanks,
> We praise you for your glory.

O Almighty and everlasting God, who
By the co-operation of the Holy Spirit
Did prepare the body and soul of Mary,
Glorious Virgin and mother,
To become the worthy dwelling of your Son;
Grant that by her gracious intercession,
In whose commemoration we rejoice,
We may be delivered from present evils
And everlasting death,
Through Jesus Christ our Lord.
Amen.

Then I heard all living things in creation – everything that lives in the air, and on the ground, and under the ground, and in the sea, crying: to the One who is sitting on the throne and to the Lamb, be all praise, honour, glory and power for ever and ever... and the four animals said 'Amen' and the elders prostrated themselves in worship.

Revelations 5:13–14

But you are a chosen race, a royal priesthood, a consecrated nation, a people set apart to sing the praises of God who called you out of the darkness into his wonderful light.

1 Peter 2:9

You shall be holy to me: for I the Lord am holy, and have separated you from the peoples, that you should be mine.

Leviticus 20:26

Dear children!
Also today I call you to renew prayer in your families. By prayer and the reading of Sacred Scripture, may the Holy Spirit, who will renew you, enter into your families. In this way, you will become teachers of the faith in your family. By prayer and love the world will set out on a better way and love will begin to rule the world. Thank you for having responded to my call.

Our Lady of Peace, Medugorje, 25 April 2005

Loaves and Fishes

31 MAY

THE VISITATION OF THE BLESSED VIRGIN MARY

The visit of the Blessed Virgin Mary to her aged cousin Elizabeth is a beautiful expression of family love and kinship.

At the sudden unexpected presence of the angel Gabriel, our Blessed Lady was deeply disturbed by his greeting: 'Rejoice, so highly favoured. The Lord is with you.'

Luke 1:28

The angel tells Mary

by the power of the Holy Spirit she is to give birth to a son, Jesus. He will be great and will be called Son of the Most High. The Lord God will give him the throne of his ancestor, David; he will rule over the house of Jacob for ever and his reign will have no end.

Luke 1:31–34

The angel had further surprising news:

Know this too: your kinswoman Elizabeth has in her old age herself conceived a son, and she whom people called barren is now in her sixth month, for nothing is impossible to God. 'I am the handmaid of the lord,' said Mary, 'let what you have said be done to me,' and the angel left her.

Luke 1:36–38

In her love for her cousin, Mary set out in deep thought as quickly as she could to be of assistance to Elizabeth in her old age.

She went into Zechariah's house and greeted Elizabeth. Now as soon as Elizabeth heard Mary's greeting, the child leapt in her womb and Elizabeth was filled with the Holy Spirit.

Luke 1:41–42

Elizabeth salutes Mary as 'Mother of God':

Why should I be honoured with a visit from the mother of my Lord? For the moment your greeting reached my ears the child in my womb leapt for joy.

Luke 1:43–44

Honour came to Elizabeth because she is visited by the Mother of God. Mary is the first to greet Elizabeth, then Elizabeth greets Mary. Inspired by the Holy Spirit, Mary exults in the words of her 'Magnificat', which falls into three sections:

1. Mary, the personification of her own people sings praise to God her Saviour.

My soul proclaims the greatness of the Lord and my spirit exults in God, my Saviour, because He has looked upon His lowly handmaid. Yes, from this day forward all generations will call me blessed, for the Almighty has done great things for me.

Luke 1:46–50

2. Mary recalls what God has done for Israel, her own people:

He has shown the power of his arm, He has routed the proud of heart. He has pulled down princes from their thrones and exalted the lowly. The hungry he has fed with good things, the rich sent away empty.

Luke 1:51–53

3. Mary sings of the divine plan foretold in Abraham and perfected in herself:

He has come to the help of Israel his servant, mindful of his mercy – according to the promise made to our ancestors – of his mercy to Abraham and to his descendants for ever.

Luke 1:54–55

In his mother's womb, John recognises Him whose herald he is to be, and who already by his Holy Spirit sanctifies John in his mother's womb. Later, John will bear witness to Jesus: 'He must increase, I must decrease.' (John 3: 30)

Seeing Jesus coming towards him, John said, 'Behold the Lamb of God who takes away the sin of the world.' (John 1:29–30)

Antiphon from the 3rd Common of the Mass of the Blessed Virgin Mary

You have been blessed, O Virgin Mary, above all other women on earth by the Lord, the most high God; for he has so exalted your name, that your praises shall never fade from the mouths of people.

Joy and the outpouring of the Holy Spirit were two signs of the advent of the Messianic era. Judith in the Old Testament saved her people and town, Bethulia, from Holofernes intent on destroying everything in his wake. She is a type of the Blessed Virgin who brought our Saviour into the world.

Visitation

May you be blessed, my daughter, by God Most High, beyond all women on earth … God grant you always to be held in honour, and rewarded with blessings, since you did not consider your own life, when our nation was brought to its knees, but warded off our ruin, walking undeterred before God.

Judith 13:24, 20–26

In the Old Testament the Ark of the Covenant symbolised God's presence among His people, a God of judgement, mercy, forgiveness, love. It contained two tablets of stone on which were inscribed the Ten Commandments. It also contained some sacred manna in a golden urn. This Ark was portable and the Israelites carried it with them in their wanderings through the wilderness. Amid great rejoicing of the people King David brought the Ark to Jerusalem, the holy city. John leapt for joy in his mother's womb, just as King David leapt before the Ark when it was brought to Jerusalem. ' "How shall the ark of the Lord come to me?" David cried.' (2 Samuel 6:9)

This is echoed by Elizabeth: 'How have I deserved the honour that the mother of my Lord should come to me?' (Luke 1:43) As the Ark of the Covenant remained in the house of Obed-Edom for three months, so did Mary remain three months in the house of Zecaharia.

Mary is the New Ark, the New Eve, because she contained within her own body, Jesus, Son of God.

We may apply to the Blessed Virgin the words of the Book of Wisdom, (7:26): 'She is a reflection of the eternal light, untarnished mirror of God's active power, image of his goodness.'

Preface 2 from the Common of the Mass of the Blessed Virgin Mary

> In celebrating the memory of the Blessed Virgin Mary, it is our special joy to echo her song of thanksgiving, what wonders you have worked throughout the world! All generations have shared in the greatness of your love.
> When you looked on Mary your lowly servant, you raised her to be the mother of Jesus Christ, your Son, our Lord, the saviour of all mankind.

Prayer after Communion on the Feast of the Visitation

> Lord, let the Church praise you for the great things you have done for your people. May we always

recognise with joy, the presence of Christ in the Eucharist we celebrate as John the Baptist hailed the presence of our Saviour in the womb of Mary.

Reflections

Among all the gifts that God has given us, our own particular family is of supreme importance. This feast of the Visitation is a graced occasion for appraising our family and also our inter-family relationships.

The family is the place where children are surrounded with love and begin to absorb human values that make for uprightness, goodness and happiness.

There is no place like a home that has been a haven of love; love which is the fullness of life, and can overcome all obstacles and turn everything into good:

...eating together as family is the salt of life.

Source unknown

Brother helped by brother is a fortress; friends are like the bars of a stronghold.

Proverbs 18:19

Practical service of others, the patience and the true affection implied, is worth more than all mortifications.

I cannot carry your pain, but when you cry, I carry your sorrow.

Source unknown

Kindly words are a honeycomb, sweet to the taste, welcome to the body.

Proverbs 16:24

As long as we love one another, God will live in us, and his love will be complete in us.

1 John 4:12

On the last day we shall be judged by our love.

> St John of the Cross, sixteenth century

The habit of family daily prayer (rosary) binds a family together in love and leads them throughout the year to partake of the Bread of Life, the Holy Eucharist, source and summit of all spiritual life.

Mary is a 'woman of the Eucharist' in her whole life. Mary, throughout her life at Christ's side and not only on Calvary, made her own the sacrificial dimension of the Eucharist. In a certain sense Mary lived her Eucharistic faith even before the institution of the Eucharist, by the very fact that she offered her virginal womb for the Incarnation of God's word.

> *Mary, Woman of the Eucharist,* Pope John Paul II

Be holy in all you do, since it is the Holy One who has called you, and scripture says: be holy, for I am holy.

> Leviticus 19:2

God is my light and my salvation, whom shall I fear? God is the fortress of my life, of whom shall I be afraid?

> Psalm 27:1

Love is the most beautiful gift you can give to anyone.
Peace always results from love.

> Father Slavko

May the Lord bless you and keep you. May the Lord let his face shine upon you and be gracious to you. May the Lord show his face to you and give you his peace.

> Numbers 6:23–24

Prayers

Let nothing disturb you,
Nothing affright you.
All things are passing,
God never changes.
Patience gains all things.

Who has God wants for nothing,
alone God suffices.

St Theresa of Avila, 1515–1582

O my Queen, O my Mother,
remember that I belong to you.
Guard me, defend me, as your
own property and possession.

To the most holy and undivided Trinity,
to the humanity of our Lord Jesus Christ
crucified, to the spotless maternity
of the most glorious ever Virgin Mary
and to the whole assembly of the saints,
be everlasting praise, honour, power
and glory from every creature, and to
us, forgiveness of all our sins,
for ever and ever.
Amen

This prayer is for recitation after the recitation of the Office of
the Blessed Virgin Mary

JUNE

MEMORIAL OF THE
IMMACULATE HEART OF MARY*

The people in our life whom we remember most are those who showed us much love in both the trivial and important events in our own life. A warm heart sheds love and creates confidence and lifts the spirits of those fortunate enough to be the object of such tenderness. The young need plenty of encouragement in their efforts to live meaningful and upright lives. They flourish when they know they are loved and valued in themselves.

The Blessed Virgin has a very pure and warm heart and loves each and all of her children unconditionally. The angel Gabriel had a very important message to deliver to her: she was loved by God in a unique way and chosen to be the mother of Emmanuel, the 'God who is with us'. For the good of all mankind she had no hesitation in accepting the angel's message. ' "I am the handmaid of the Lord. Let what you have said be done to me." And the angel left her.' (Luke 1:38) Her answer was simple, direct, complete and came from a most loving heart.

So our Mother hurried off to visit and assist her aged cousin, Elizabeth, whom she made very happy with her greeting and presence: 'Why should I be honoured with a visit from the mother of my Lord?' (Luke 1:43)

Elizabeth welcomes the visit of her cousin, the Virgin Mary, whose heart breaks forth in her beautiful canticle, 'Magnificat', a canticle of praise and thanksgiving for the mercies of God: 'My soul proclaims the greatness of the Lord and my spirit exults in God my saviour.' (Luke 1:46)

---

* Saturday following the second Sunday after Pentecost

At the marriage feast at Cana, the blessed Virgin seems to have been the principal guest for St John notes firstly that the '...Mother of Jesus was there.' Then only does he mention that '...Jesus and his disciples had also been invited.' (John 2:1)

Our Blessed Lady quickly perceives that 'they ran out of wine'. (John 2:3) To save their hosts from embarrassment, Our Lady turns to her son, Jesus, for help and is not disappointed. The steward tells the bridegroom, 'You have kept the best wine till now.' (John 2:10) All those with a loving heart have always something more to give.

But the heart of our Mother Mary also had disappointments and sorrows. When her time had come, there was no one willing in Bethlehem to offer shelter to her and Joseph. While their most loving heart rejoiced at the birth of Jesus and was grateful for the visit of the shepherds and the wise men from the East, there was also a feeling of anxiety over their unexpected flight into Egypt. In the Temple, Simeon prophesised that Mary's Child would be a 'sign that is rejected – and a sword will pierce your own soul too – so that the secret thoughts of many may be laid bare.' (Luke 2:35)

The Virgin Mother's most loving heart must have been distraught by the disappearance of their twelve-year-old son, Jesus. It is true that love becomes perfect in suffering.

> 'My child, why have you do this to us? See how worried your father and I have been looking for you?'
>
> 'Why were you looking for me?' he replied. 'Did you not know that I must be about my father's affairs?' But they did not understand what he meant. His mother stored up all these things in her heart.
>
> Luke 2:49–51

Love accepts the inevitable and finds another way to reach the truth.

A great silence covers the years when Jesus grew to manhood and learned the carpenter's trade from St Joseph. This silence was an interior withdrawal in preparation for the arduous years of Jesus' public life. But in these intimate and hidden years the hearts of Jesus, Mary and Joseph were bound together in deep eternal love.

After rejecting Satan's temptation during his forty days' fast in the wilderness we are told that:

> Jesus, with the power of the Spirit in him, returned to Galilee; and his reputation spread throughout the countryside. He taught in their synagogues and everyone praised him.
>
> Luke 4:14–15

The heart of His mother would have rejoiced at this but would have been very troubled at His being expelled from Nazareth when He spoke words favourable to the Gentiles (the widow at Zarephath & Naaman the Syrian in Luke 4:16–30).

It's possible that our Blessed Mother was among the crowd that witnessed the public trial of Jesus before Pilate.

Her loving heart must have been sorely afflicted and especially at the Cross of Calvary where, along with St John, her heart compassionately shared in Jesus' sufferings.

> All you who pass this way look and see: is any sorrow like the sorrow that afflicts me?
>
> Jeremiah 1:12

It may well be that the Virgin Mother was the very first person to be greeted by her Son at His Resurrection – a meeting too intimate to find its way into any of the four gospels, and a convergence of two most loving hearts.

Our Blessed Lady was taken body and soul into heaven for the earth was not worthy to receive her and there was no one in the world that had a heart so full of love for her Divine Son and for all of us.

> We take into ourselves the love of the Sacred Heart of Jesus for us, our veneration for our Blessed Mother is an undying tribute to her love for Jesus and St Joseph and all of us her children.
>
> She is the Immaculate Mother whose heart overflows with full undying love for all God's children here on earth.
>
> The entire holiness and love of the Mother of God pours out from her Immaculate Heart, a Heart that is the focused symbol of love for all her sinful children.

Love in all its dimensions is the most beautiful gift our Blessed Mother gives us for then we are free, courageous and partakers of the Divine Life of Jesus for ever.

2 Peter 2:1–4

Above all, let us listen to Mary Most Holy in whom the mystery of the Eucharist appears, more than in anyone else, as a mystery of light. Gazing upon Mary, we come to know the transforming power present in the Eucharist. In her we see the world renewed in love.

Contemplating her, assumed body and soul into heaven, we see opening before us 'new heavens' and those 'new earths' which will appear at the second coming of Christ.

Here below, the Eucharist represents their pledge and in a certain way, their anticipation. In the humble signs of bread and wine, changed into his body and blood, Christ walks beside us as our strength and our food for the journey, and he enables us to become, for everyone, witnesses of hope.

Pope John Paul II of Blessed Memory, *Ecclesia de Eucharistia*

Immaculate Heart

God does not see as man sees; man looks at appearances, but God looks at the heart.

1 Samuel 16:7

As for Mary, she treasured all these things and pondered them in her heart.

Luke 2:19

A good man draws what is good from the store of goodness in his heart.

Luke 6:45

Hail to Thee, true body sprung
From the Virgin Mary's womb
The same that on the cross was hung,
And bore for man the bitter doom.

Thou whose side was pierced, and flowed
Both with water and with blood,
Suffer us to taste of Thee
in our life's last agony.

O kind, O Loving One!
Sweet Jesus, Mary's Son.

We fly to thy patronage,
O Holy Mother of God;
despise not our prayers in
our necessities,
but deliver us from all dangers,
O ever glorious and Blessed
Virgin.

Third century prayer in the Roman catacombs

Dear children!
Also today I call you to pray, pray, pray. Little children, when you pray, you are close to God and He gives you the desire for eternity. This is a time when you can speak more about God and do more for God. Therefore, little children, do not rest but permit Him to lead you, to change you and to enter into your life. Do not forget that you are travellers on the way toward eternity. Therefore, little children, permit God to lead you as a shepherd leads his flock. Thank you for having responded to my call.

Our Lady of Peace, Medugorje, 25 November 2006

Conclusion

Our good Mother, the eternal Virgin Mary, never preached a sermon in the synagogue or in the marketplace.

But she speaks to our heart directly from her own all-loving heart by her example of readiness to do God's will, to deal with uncertainties, always at peace, modest in bearing, humble in action, compassionate to the discomfited newly-weds, patient in suffering, happy in her life of service to Jesus and St Joseph.

By her example, Mary our Mother speaks directly from her heart to our heart. All of us who are seeking the ultimate truth hear her whisper to us, 'Don't be afraid! My Son Jesus loves you beyond all reckoning, well beyond anything you can imagine! And I, your Mother, love you with all my heart.'

David and Goliath

Copyright © John August Swanson 2005

16 JULY

OUR LADY OF MOUNT CARMEL

ount Carmel in northern Palestine rises to a height of 1,800 feet above sea level, overlooks the Mediterranean and in biblical times was covered in magnificent forests.

It was a mountain sacred to the prophet Elijah (875 BC) and chosen as the site of the altar in the contest between him and the prophets of Baal, to determine which deity would end the long drought over the land. The consumption of the sacrificial bull by the fire he called down was proof that God alone is the God of the rain and of the whole world. Elijah had raised a widow's son from death, was fed by ravens on his long trek to Horeb (also called Sinai), where he had the experience of '...the still small voice of God', a sound of sheer silence. He departed this life on a chariot of fire in a sweeping whirlwind.

Elijah appeared with Moses conversing with Jesus in His transfiguration: '...they were speaking of his passing (Jesus') which He was to accomplish in Jerusalem.' (Luke 9:31)

Made sacred by the presence of Elijah, Mount Carmel was noted for its beauty, fertility and its numerous caves suitable for hermits leading a contemplative life. A group of hermits settled on this holy mountain in the twelfth century and they became known as the Brethren of Blessed Mary of Mount Carmel. A century later, St Simon Stock of Alyseford, Kent, was given a brown scapular by our Blessed Lady to be worn as a guarantee of her help in our times of need. Its fame spread into modern times and is one of the oldest devotions in the Church, replaced now by the scapular medal.

The original scapular was a garment with an opening for the head and hanging down in front and behind the body. Several orders adopted the original scapular as a monastic dress, such as the Benedictines, Dominicans and so on.

Carmelite life is marked by collective and individual solitude. This induces an atmosphere in which union with God is achieved by constant prayer in the spirit of Elijah and our Blessed Lady of Mount Carmel. In our own times the contemplative spirit is the inspiration of their present apostolic activity. 'I live, now not I, but Christ lives in me.' (Galatians 20)

In the fourteenth century an order of Carmelite nuns came into being. They lived in small communities of enclosed contemplative life with the desire to assist the Carmelite friars by their prayerful life and penances. Probably the best known Carmelites of our own day are: St Teresa of Avila (sixteenth century), St John of the Cross (sixteenth century), St Therese of Lisieux (nineteenth century) and St Edith Stein (Sister Benedicta of the Cross, twentieth century).

St Teresa wrote a great deal about prayer:

> Anyone who has not begun to pray, I beg, for love of the Lord, not to miss so great blessing … and mental (inner) prayer in my view, is nothing other but a friendly conversation with the Lord … frequent solitary conversations with Him whom we know loves us.

St John of the Cross became a Carmelite at the age of fifteen. He is Spain's greatest poet and his teachings on prayer are really commentaries on his mystical (spiritual) poetry.

He constantly urges the need to purify the soul by mortification of the body and by accepting in peace unsought humiliations. We must live for God alone in order to know Him as the God of love for the thirsting soul. St John is a master of contemplative prayer.

St Therese of Lisieux entered the Carmelite order at the age of fifteen. Later the prioress (her own sister Pauline) asked Therese to write out her life story, which Therese called *The Story of the Springtime of a Little White Flower*. This book made St Therese famous all over the world. Before her death she suffered greatly in body and spirit and died at the age of twenty-four. She had a wonderful gift for explaining her ideals in a most simple clear way. Her way was the way of 'spiritual childhood' which she described as the 'Little Way'. She confessed,

I have always been looking for a lift by which I may raise myself to God, for I am too small to climb the stairway to perfection ... I feel my mission is soon to begin ... to teach souls my little way. I will spend my time in heaven in doing good on earth.

St Edith Stein (Sister Benedicta of the Cross), a convert Jew, became a Carmelite nun at the age of forty-two.

Both her conversion and her entry into Carmel were a very sore trial for her mother, whom Edith loved so tenderly. For Edith, her Catholicism was not a denial of her faith but its complete fulfilment. From Echt in Holland she was transported with her sister, Rosa, to the concentration camp of Auschwitz. On her way to the gas ovens she said to her sister, Rosa, 'Let us go and suffer for our people.' This was on 9 August 1942. Indeed, Sister Benedicta's sacrifice along with her sister, Rosa, was a sacrifice made for the redemption of all peoples through the crucified Christ of Calvary. Sister Benedicta had a brilliant mind: a notable philosopher, she is one of the most remarkable and intellectual saints of the twentieth century.

Satan will not come near to molest any person who is wearing the scapular or scapular medal or any blessed insignia. Such an article is a symbol reminding us of who we are, souls created in God's image and likeness. The struggle against evil is a warfare in which we are all engaged. St Paul urges us '...to grow strong in the Lord, with the strength of his power. Put on God's armour to be able to resist the devil's tactics.' (Ephesians 6:10–12)

All these symbols are related to Christ and his Blessed Mother and reinforce the gospel message to pray unceasingly. They are silent witnesses of our love of Jesus and the Blessed Virgin whose heart overflows with maternal love for all of us, her children. She is the great sign of God's love for us as we participate with her Divine Son in the salvation of the world.

In wearing sacred insignia we glorify our Lord and His holy Mother and in our heart's memory we cherish their presence in our daily lives.

These insignia are also a reminder of our sacramental life, especially the Holy Eucharist, The Living Bread of Life.

Mary can guide us towards this most holy sacrament, because she herself has a profound relationship with it ... Gazing upon Mary, we come to know the transforming power present in the Eucharist.

Ecclesia de Eucharistia, Pope John Paul II

Carrying on our person, say, the 'Miraculous Medal' can help remind us of the supreme importance of keeping the Sunday holy. When we ponder, O Christ, the marvels accomplished on this day, the Sunday of your holy Resurrection, we say:

Blessed is Sunday ... for on it began creation ... the world's salvation ... the renewal of the human race ... on Sunday heaven and earth rejoiced and the whole universe was filled with light. Blessed is Sunday, for on it were opened the gates of paradise so that Adam and all the exiles might enter it without fear.

Syriac Office of Antioch, Catechism of
the Catholic Church, no. 1167

One thing took deep root in me – the conviction that morality is the basis of things, and that truth is the substance of morality.

The vitality of a society is bound up with its religion. It is the religious impulse which supplies the cohesive force which unifies a society and culture.

The great religions are the foundation on which the great civilisations rest.

A society which has lost its religion becomes sooner or later a society which has lost its culture.

Words of Wisdom from Mahatma Gandhi

Knowledge is power, wisdom is freedom. God give me the great and mighty calm that pervades all nature.

Etty Hillesum, 1914–1943

Contrition is the daily bread of all spiritual people.

Quote from the Desert Fathers, fourth century

This is my commandment: love one another, as I have loved you.

John 15:12

Hail, holy Queen, Mother of mercy,
Hail, our life, our sweetness and our hope.
To you do we cry, poor banished
children of Eve.
To you do we send up our sighs,
mourning and weeping in this
vale of tears.
Turn then, most gracious advocate,
Your eyes of mercy towards us,
and after this, our exile, show
unto us the blessed fruit
of your womb, Jesus.
O clement, O loving, O sweet
Virgin Mary.
Let us pray.

Dear Children!
I call you anew; be open to my messages. I desire, little children, to draw you all closer to my Son, Jesus; therefore, you pray and fast. Especially, I call you to pray for my intentions, so that I can present you to my Son Jesus for him to transform and open your hearts to love. When you will have love in the heart, peace will rule in you. Thank you for having responded to my call.'

Our Lady Queen of Peace, Medugorje, 15 July 2004

Our Lady of Mount Carmel, pray for us. Blessed be the great Mother of God, Mary most holy. Blessed be her holy and immaculate conception. Blessed be her glorious Assumption. Blessed be the name of Mary, Virgin and Mother. Blessed be St Joseph her spouse most chaste. Blessed be God in his angels and in his saints.

15 August

Solemnity of the Assumption

he life of the holy Mother of God, like that of so many ordinary people, was marked by extreme simplicity in the silence of obscurity and the beauty of holiness. It was fitting that Mary's conception be protected by marriage and so be justified in the eyes of the world. Only Mary knew the provenance of her divine conception but kept it secret in the depths of her heart. Being conscious of her innocence she remained calm and peaceful and committed to God the righteous judge. St Joseph was sorely perplexed by Mary's condition but chose to remain silent rather than make of her a public example. He was a just man, not willing to expose her, but rather to put her away privately. God, however, intervened and sent an angel to direct Joseph to his intended marriage with Mary because:

> ...she has conceived what is in her by the Holy Spirit. She will give birth to a son and you must name him Jesus, because he is the one to save the people from their sins ... the child will be called Emmanuel.

> Matthew 1:18–24

In St Luke's gospel Mary asks the angel for more information: 'How can this come about since I am a virgin?' She is informed, at that moment, of Elizabeth's conception, 'For nothing is impossible to God.' Mary answered simply and humbly: 'I am the handmaid of the Lord, let what you have said be done to me.' (Luke 1:37–38)

Elizabeth praises Mary (who in a sense has become a public person) for her faith. 'Yes, from this day forward all generations will call me blessed, for the Almighty has done great things for me.' (Luke 1:48) The words of Mary's Magnificat resound each day round the world in the divine liturgy.

> The wise men, the kings from the East, found the infant king of the Jews in his mother's arms and, falling on their knees, they did him homage, presented their rich gifts and left in silence, never to be heard of again.

Seeking asylum in Egypt, the Holy Family pre-empted the twenty-first-century phenomenon of immigration from middle Europe, Asia and Africa, of people seeking work and their daily bread in the more affluent West.

Mary and Joseph experienced alternate joys and sorrows just as people face them in their ordinary lives. They had an experience of loss not uncommon today: they lost their twelve-year-old child and were unable to understand why He said: 'Did you not know that I must be about my father's affairs?' (Luke 2:49)

Grieving in silence, the sword predicted by Simeon in the Temple was beginning to pierce Mary's heart. It was Mary who was the first to note the immanent embarrassment of the bridal pair at Cana when the wine ran out. In faith, His mother said to the servants, 'Do whatever he tells you!' Jesus did not disappoint His Mother or the assembled guests. He '...let his glory be seen, and his disciples believed in him.' (John 2:11)

> On the threshold of his public life Jesus performs his first sign – at his mother's request – during a wedding feast. The Church attaches great importance to Jesus' presence at the wedding at Cana. It is seen as a confirmation of the goodness of marriage and the proclamation that henceforth marriage will be an efficacious sign of Christ's presence.
>
> Catechism of the Catholic Church, no. 1613

In the silent years from Cana to Calvary the Blessed Virgin looked after the home and, as a mother, performed the usual household chores like all the other women in the neighbourhood. In the quietness of the family home, along with Jesus and Joseph she would be praying, reading the scriptures and attending the synagogue with them for public prayer.

At the last Passover in Jesus' life she may have been in the crowd witnessing the public trial of Jesus before Pilate in compassionate silence. Perhaps his mother was with the 'women of Jerusalem' as they walked with Jesus to Calvary, where at the foot of the cross with John 'the beloved disciple', she suffered intensely.

Millions and millions of people have lived since the time of Adam and Eve, but only one of them was without sin, and that person was a woman, and that woman was the blessed Virgin Mary, the holy Mother of God. All women should be especially proud that one of their number was chosen by God from all eternity to be absolutely sinless and unique as the Mother of our Lord Jesus Christ.

Mary embodies the tenderness of silent love that is unconditional. Countries north, south, east and west have each their own ethnic figure of Mary because she belongs to all people everywhere. The human body was utterly degraded in the gas chambers and furnaces of Auschwitz and Belsen. But God Himself honoured the human body by becoming one of us through an earthly Mother, whose body was glorified by being assumed into heaven, for Adam's sin had never touched her.

> Now a great sign appeared in heaven: a woman adorned with the sun, standing on the moon, with twelve stars on her head for a crown.

> Revelations 12:1

Mary shines with the light of her divine son, as fair as the moon, with all the apostles and saints attending. Our own mortal bodies on the Last Day will shine and live with Jesus, Mary and Joseph for ever and ever. The very cycle of nature itself is a symbol of our passage from birth to life and, ultimately, our birth into immortality. Jesus Himself assures us: 'Anyone who does eat my flesh and drinks my blood, has eternal life, and I shall raise him up on the last day.' (John 6:54)

The Blessed Virgin is one of us but in an entirely unique way. Her glorious assumption reinforces the teaching of St Paul:

Your body you know, is the temple of the Holy Spirit, who is in you since you received him from God. You are not your own property; you have been bought and paid for. That is why you should use your body for the glory of God.

1 Corinthians 6:19–20

The human body shares in the dignity of the 'image of God': it is a human body because it is animated by a spiritual soul, and it is the whole person that is intended to become, in the body of Christ, a temple of the Spirit.

Catechism of the Catholic Church, no. 364

Purity requires modesty, an integral part of temperance. Modesty protects the intimate centre of a person. It means refusing to unveil what should remain hidden. It is ordered to chastity to whose sensitivity it bears witness. It guides how one looks at others and behaves towards them in conformity with the dignity of persons and their solidarity.

Catechism of Catholic Church, no 2521

Modesty is decency. It inspires one's choice of clothing. It keeps silence or reserve where there is evident risk of unhealthy curiosity. It is discreet.

Catechism of the Catholic Church, no. 2522

Prayer from the Vigil Mass

Let us pray with Mary to the Father in whose presence she now dwells.
Almighty Father of our Lord Jesus Christ, you have revealed the beauty of your power by exalting the lowly virgin of Nazareth and making her the mother of our Saviour. May the prayers of this woman clothed with the sun bring Jesus to the waiting world and fill the void of incompletion with the presence of her child who lives and reigns with you and the Holy spirit, for ever and ever.

Dear Children!

Also today I call you to pray, pray, pray. Only in prayer will you be near to me and my Son and you will come to see how short this life is. In your heart a desire for heaven will be born. Joy will begin to rule in your heart and prayer will begin to flow like a river. In your words there will only be thanksgiving to God for having created you and the desire for holiness will become a reality for you. Thank you for having responded to my call.

Our Lady Queen of Peace Medugorje 25 August 2006

Conclusion

The Feasts of the liturgical year are invitations for intensification of our prayer and worship '...as partakers of the divine nature.' (2 Peter 1:4)

To converse habitually with our Lord, whose kingdom is within us, gives a self-containment and self-confidence that is peaceful, happy and loving. We should pray everywhere and on every occasion – praying from the heart, especially in thanksgiving for all that God has given us in sorrow and joy, in tears and in laughter. Morning, noon and evening we should pray as well as when we awaken during the night. The prayer that comes from our hearts as we go about our normal activities teaches us how to love and forgive; a love that feels for the sufferings of people and the whole world. Prayer fuels the divine discontent within us but brings calm and healing and an assurance that the Lord is truly with us in all our brokenness and frailty. Love creates space for prayer in freedom from harmful anxieties and worries. Prayer is the breath of the soul, breathing with the Holy Spirit, night and day. Remember to pray on every occasion and close the day with the gentle peace of the rosary. Like Moses on Mount Sinai, St Peter declared:

> but you are a chosen race, a royal priesthood, a consecrated nation, a people set apart to sing the praises of God.

Peter 1:4

This is what God asks of you: only this, to act justly, to love tenderly, and to walk humbly with your God.

Micah 6:8

Do not be afraid, for I have redeemed you. I have called you by your name, you are mine.

Isaiah 43:1

Should you pass through the sea, I will be with you; or through rivers, they will not swallow you up. Should you walk through fire, you will not be scorched and the flames will not burn you. For I am Yahweh your God, the Holy One of Israel, your Saviour.

Isaiah 43:1–3

22 August

Memorial of the Queenship of Mary

his Feast was instituted by Pope Pius XII in 1954:

> …so that all may more clearly recognize and venerate the kind and maternal role of the Mother of God.

> Finally, preserved from all guilt of original sin, the immaculate Virgin was taken up body and soul into heavenly glory upon the completion of her earthly sojourn.

Lumen Gentium: Vat II The Dogmatic Constitution of the Church
no. 59

From the Daily Prayer of the Divine Office
Our Lady Queen and Mother

Invitatory Antiphon

> Christ, the king, crowned His Mother as Queen of heaven.
> Come let us adore Him.

Benedictus antiphon

> Hail, O Queen of all the world, ever Virgin Mary.
> You bore Christ the Lord, the Saviour of all creation.

Psalm 45:10

Upon your right hand stands the Queen in gold of Ophir.*

Litany of Loreto (Litany of our Lady)

In this litany our Mother Mary is addressed twelve times in terms that affirm the nature and extent of her Queenship.

> Queen on whose starry brow doth rest
> The crown of perfect maidenhood
> The God who made thee, from thy breast
> Draws for our sakes, his earthly food.

Venantius Fortunatus, fifth century

1. Regina Angelorum
Queen of Angels

The angels, spirit by nature, are the messengers of God.

> In the sixth month the angel Gabriel was sent by God to a town in Galilee called Nazareth to announce to Mary that God had chosen her to become the Mother of our Redeemer.

Luke 1:25

> The angel of the Lord appeared to the shepherds and the glory of the Lord shone round about them. They were terrified, but the angel said: 'Do not be afraid, I bring you news of great joy to be shared by the whole people. Today, in the town of David, a saviour has been born to you; he is Christ the Lord.'

Luke 2:9–12

From the Incarnation to the Ascension the life of the Word incarnate is surrounded by the adoration and service of angels.

---

* Ophir was a land of fabulous wealth, possibly in south east Arabia, from where King Solomon's fleet brought back hordes of gold.

When He brings his first-born into the world, He says, 'Let all the angels worship him.'

Hebrews 1:6

Their song of praise at the birth of Christ has not ceased resounding in the Church's praise: 'Glory to God in the highest'. (Luke 2:14)

They protect Jesus in his infancy, serve Him in the desert, strengthen Him in His agony in the garden, when He could have been saved by them from the hands of His enemies.

Again it is the angels who evangelise by proclaiming the Good News of Christ's Incarnation and Resurrection. 'He is risen. He is not here.'

Mark 16:5–7

They will be present at Christ's return which they will announce to serve at His judgement.

Catechism of the Catholic Church, no. 333

You have willed to crown the Mother of Christ with a royal diadem so that she could more clearly demonstrate to her children her benevolence and love.

Preface of the Mass for the Feast of the Queenship of Mary.

2. Regina Patriarcharum
Queen of Patriarchs

In the Old Testament, the patriarchs such as Moses, Abraham, Isaac, Jacob and so on, were leaders and guides of their peoples and have always been venerated as special friends of God. St Joseph, husband of Mary, foster father of the Son of God and protector of the universal Church is truly the last of the great patriarchs.

Hail Mary, full of grace and Queen of Patriarchs, pray for us.

3. Regina Prophetarum
Queen of Prophets

In the Old Testament times there were about seventy recognized prophets. The prophets foretold the birth, passion, sufferings and death and the final glory and triumph of the Redeemer. Zechariah prophesised that his son John would become the 'Prophet of the Most High' and '…prepare his way before Him'. (Luke 1:67, 76)

Mary our Mother had the gift of prophecy.

Henceforth all generations will call me blessed.

Luke 1:48

She is the tree of life for those who hold her fast;
    Those who cling to her live happy lives.

Proverbs 3:18

She knows the past, she forecasts the future…
    She has fore knowledge of signs and wonders
    The unfolding of the ages and the times.

Wisdom 8:8

4. Regina Apostolorum
Queen of Apostles

At Cana of Galilee Jesus told His Mother, 'My hour has not yet come.' But His Mother said to the servants, 'Do whatever he tells you … he let his glory be seen, and his disciples believed in Him.' (John 2:5–12)

For she is an inexhaustible treasure to men, and those who acquire it win God's friendship, commended as they are to him by the benefits of her teaching.

Wisdom 7:13–14

St Gregory of Tours (sixth century) relates:

> When the blessed Mary had fulfilled the course of this present life and was now to be called out of this world, all the apostles were gathered together from several regions to her house. As they learnt that she was to be taken from the world, together they watched her, when behold, Jesus arrived with his angels, and receiving her soul committed her to the archangel Michael, and then withdrew.

St John Damascene (eighth century):

> Would not they who after the Ascension of their Master returned to Jerusalem rejoicing, do likewise on this occasion, and disperse to their various missions feeling Mary was no longer not only their Mother, but their heavenly Queen, watching over, pleading for and waiting for the day to come when she would welcome them with joy and magnificence to the kingdom.

5. Regina Martyrum
Queen of Martyrs

A Christian martyr is one who sacrifices his or her life in bearing witness to his faith in Jesus Christ, and is a witness of the Gospel teaching in his resolution to follow Jesus who came to bear witness to the truth: 'I have come to bear witness to the truth and all those who are on the side of truth listen to my voice.' (John 18:37)

The martyr unflinchingly chooses death with all its cruelties rather than deny Christ. The martyr is a witness to the eternal truth given to us by our Lord Jesus Christ in His life, death and Resurrection.

> They loved not their lives even unto death.
>
> Revelations 12:11

> Happy are those who are persecuted in the cause of right; theirs is the kingdom of heaven … Rejoice and be glad for your reward

will be great in heaven. This is how they persecuted the prophets before you.

Matthew 5:10–12

You see this child; he is destined for the fall and the rising of many in Israel, destined to be a sign that is rejected and a sword will pierce your own soul too – so that the secret of many hearts may be revealed.

Luke 2:34–35

Mary, Mother of Jesus, must have been aware of the opposition of the Pharisees and Sadducees. During the fatal week of Jesus' final Passover, she would have known about His arrest, trial, scourging, crowning with thorns, and would have witnessed His most painful carrying of the cross to Calvary.

My people what have I done to you? How have I offended you? Answer me.

Micah 6:3

Near the cross stood His Mother and His Mother's sister, Mary of Cleopas, and Mary Magdala.

John 19:25

At the cross her station keeping,
    Stood the mournful mother weeping,
    Close to Jesus to the last.

Stabat Mater

All you who pass this way
    Look and see is any sorrow like my sorrow
    With which Yahweh has struck me
    On this day of burning anger.

Lamentations 1:12

In the penal times of Henry VIII (1491–1547), Queen Elizabeth (1533–1603) and James VI (1566–1625) Great Britain had two hundred and sixty martyrs.

In our violent world of today not a few parents are weeping in the mood of King David:

81

My son Absalom! My son! Would I had died in your place!
O Absalom my son, my son!

Samuel 18:33

6. Regina Confessorum
Queen of Confessors

A Confessor is one who professes faith openly in a life distinguished by holiness.

This title is applied to all saints who are not martyrs.

Our baptismal vocation in this world is to know, love and serve God and so come to heaven as '...partakers in the divine nature.' (2 Peter 1:4)

So if anyone declares himself/herself for me in the presence of the whole world, I will declare myself for him/her in the presence of my Father in heaven.

Matthew 10:32

You are the light of the world ... In the same way your light must shine in the sight of the world, so that seeing your good works, they may give praise to your Father in heaven.

Matthew 5:14–16

Yet, you have made him little less than a god; with glory and honour you crowned him, gave him power over the works of your hand, put all things under his feet.

Psalm 8:6–7

Listen, O heavens, and I will speak, let the earth hear the words on my lips. May my teaching fall like the rain, my speech descend like the dew, like rain drops on the young green, like showers falling on the grass.

Deuteronomy 32:1–12

Many great saints have the title of Confessor, such as:

St Ninian (fifth century)

St Margaret, Queen of Scotland (eleventh century)

Bernard of Clairvaux (twelfth century)

St Vincent de Paul (seventeenth century)

St John Mary Vianney, Curé of Ars (nineteenth century)

and many others.

7. Regina Virginum
Queen of Virgins
Queen of Celibate Consecrated Life

The Book of Wisdom urges us to love virtue:

> Seek the Lord in simplicity of heart, since he is to be found by those who do not put him to the test.

> Wisdom 1:1

Some Pharisees set about questioning Jesus about divorce and in Matthew 19:1–12, Jesus condemns divorce outright.

Some take on a life of virginity for the sake of the kingdom of heaven, but, He adds, 'It is not everyone who can accept what I have said [about virginity] but only those to whom it is granted.'

When virginity is a voluntary choice for the kingdom of heaven it normally implies the consecration of a vow in a monastic or religious community. It is a special grace and vocation. It requires a lifelong generosity in the service of God and a sincere aspiration for life in the kingdom of God.

In heaven persons will not marry because they will not die. In this respect they will be like the angels. This aspect of consecrated life helps us to appreciate the vocation of our Blessed Lady in its complete integrity.

The beauty of the king's daughter is all glorious within; her clothing is of wrought gold.

Psalm 45:13

In historical pagan religions, a young virgin woman was treated with respect. She appeared a symbol of freshness and purity and a kind of youthful integrity of the forces of life.

None can doubt that she who is Queen will be the foremost of all to sing that song, which it will be given to virgins alone to sing in the kingdom of God … hers will be the sweetest and clearest voice, whose notes will make glad the city of our God.

St Bernard of Clairveaux, twelfth century

8. Regina Sanctorum Omnium
Queen of All Saints

In the midst of her own people she shall be exalted and shall be admired in the whole assembly.

Wisdom 24:2

From all eternity in the beginning, he created me, and for eternity I shall remain.

Wisdom 24:14

I have taken root in an honourable people, in the Lord's property, in his inheritance.

Wisdom 24:16

All that is beautiful and true and praiseworthy exists in heaven in all its plenitude.

One thing I have desired of the Lord, and I will seek after; that I may dwell in the house of the Lord all the days of my life to behold the beauty of the Lord, and to live in his temple.

Psalm 27:4

In her Magnificat the Blessed Virgin tells us the source of her own holiness:

> My soul proclaims the greatness of the Lord and my spirit exults in God my saviour because he has looked upon his lowly handmaid.
>
> Yes, from this day forward all generations will call me blessed, for the Almighty has done great things for me.

Luke 1:46–49

> Holiness ever befits your dwelling.

Psalm 93:5

> We fly to thy patronage, O Holy Mother of God; despise not our prayers in our necessities, but deliver us from all dangers, O ever glorious and blessed Virgin.

Third century

Queen of all saints, pray for us!

9. Regina sine Labe Originali Concepta
Queen Conceived without Original Sin

> How beautiful you are my love. How beautiful you are!

Song of Songs 1:15

> Hail Mary, full of grace, the Lord is with thee.
>   Blessed art thou among women
>   And blessed is the fruit of thy womb, Jesus.

> Thou art all fair my love, and there is no spot in thee.

Song of Songs 4:7

Preface for the Feast of the Immaculate Conception:

> You allowed no stain of Adam's sin to touch the Virgin Mary.
>   Full of grace, she was to be a worthy mother of your Son,

Your sign of favour to the Church in its beginning,
And the promise of its perfection as the bride of Christ, radiant in beauty.
Mary's sinlessness is a triumph of God's power, honour for herself,
And a glory for the whole human race

The Father blessed Mary more than any other created person
in Christ with every spiritual blessing from heaven
and chose her in Christ before the foundation of the world to
be holy and blameless before him in love.

Catechism of the Catholic Church, no. 492

Because of our inherited original sin all of us are prone to wrongdoing and evil.

Mary, our blessed Mother, is the only human being free from all temptation to sin, and so is given power as the Refuge of the sinners.

10. Regina Sacratissimi Rosarii Queen of the Most Holy Rosary

The rosary is a reflection on and a contemplating of the great truths of our faith.

The joyful mysteries concern the wonders of the Incarnation; the sorrowful; our Lord's sufferings and death; the glorious mysteries: the Resurrection and the Assumption of the Blessed Virgin into heaven.

It is a biblical prayer, simple and gently rhythmical in its repetition of the Hail Mary and the Lord's Prayer.

The 'Glory be...' at the end of each decade reminds us: 'My soul gives thanks to the lord and never forgets all his blessings.' (Psalm 103:2)

The rosary was little St Bernadette Soubirous' favourite prayer: Our Blessed Lady would appear to her holding her rosary on her arm, and pass the rosary through her fingers as Bernadette prayed the Hail Marys.

Dear children!
Also in this peaceless time, I call you to prayer.
Little children pray for peace so that every person in
the world would feel love towards peace. Only
when the soul finds peace in God does it feel con-
tent and love will then begin to flow in the world.
And in a special way, little children, you are called
to live and witness peace – peace in your hearts and
families, and through you, peace will also begin to
flow in the world. Thank you for having responded
to my call.

Our Lady of Peace, Medugorje, 25 September 2002

Mary crowned with living light,
Temple of the Lord,
Place of Peace and holiness,
Shelter of the Word.

The victories over the armed forces of Islam who were
endeavouring to invade Europe at Lepanto, Greece on 7 October
1571, at Belgrade in 1456 and Vienna in 1683 were attributed by
the Christian forces to their praying the rosary for the safety and
wellbeing of homeland Europe.

He that is mighty has done great things for me.

Luke 1:49

And so with great confidence we also pray:
Holy Mary, Mother of God,
pray for us sinners,
now and at the hour of our death.
Amen.

11. Regina Pacis
Queen of Peace

Great peace have they who love your law.

Psalm 118:165

Great is the Lord who takes pleasure in the peace of his servant.

Psalm 35:27

Peace is the tranquillity of order.

St Augustine, fifth Century

And the work of Justice shall be peace, and the service of justness, quietness and security for ever.

Isaiah 32:17

In the evening of the same day, the first day of the week, the doors were closed where the disciples were. He said to them: 'Peace be with you.' And showed them his hands and his side. The disciples were filled with joy when they saw the Lord, and He said to them again, 'Peace be with you.'

John 21:20–21

True peace and happiness depends on our inner peace and contentment which are fruits of the Holy Spirit: love, joy, peace, patience, kindness, goodness, faithfulness, gentleness and self-control, as is stated in Galatians 5:22.

And suddenly with the angel was a great throng of the heavenly host, praising God and singing: 'Glory to God in the highest, and on earth peace to men of good will.

Luke 2:14

Blessed are the peacemakers for they shall be called the children of God.

Matthew 5:9

Isaiah the prophet (ninth century BC) foretold the coming of Jesus, 'The Prince of Peace.' (9:6)

In the fourteenth century, Blessed Henry Suso prayed: 'O, Mary, what must thyself be, since the very name is so amiable and gracious.'

> You cannot be named without inflaming the heart of the person who does so, with love of you.
>
> St Bernard of Clairvaux, twelfth century

There are several historical hymns in honour of the Queenship of the Blessed Virgin Mary, composed in Latin, the language of the universal Church.

'Salve Regina'
'Hail Queen of Heaven'
(monastic in origin)

> Hail, holy Queen, Mother of mercy,
> Hail, our life, our sweetness and our hope.
> To thee do we cry, poor banished children of Eve;
> To thee do we send up our sighs,
> Mourning and weeping in this vale of tears.
> Turn then, most gracious advocate,
> Thine eyes of mercy towards us;
> And after this our exile, show unto us
> The blessed fruit of thy womb, Jesus,
> O Clement, O loving, O sweet Virgin Mary.

It was St Bernard of Clairvaux (twelfth century) who, in the Cathedral of Spiers, in a burst of fervour, added the three last invocations at the end of this prayer.

Ave Maris Stella (ninth century)

> Hail, thou star of ocean, portal of the sky,
> Every virgin Mother of the Lord most high...

Regina Caeli, Queen of Heaven, (thirteenth century)

> Queen of heaven rejoice, alleluia,
> For He whom you were worthy to bear, alleluia,
> Has risen as He said, alleluia,
> Pray for us to God, alleluia.

> Let us pray.
> O God who gave joy to the whole world through
> the resurrection of your Son, our Lord Jesus Christ,
> grant that we may obtain through his Virgin Mother
> the joys of everlasting life, through the same Christ,
> our Lord.
> Amen.

Ave Regina Caelorum (twelfth century)

> Hail, Queen of Heaven, beyond compare,
> To whom the angels homage pay;
> Hail root of Jesse, Gate of light,
> That opened for the world's new day.

Stanbrooke Abbey Hymnal

Geoffrey Chaucer (fourteenth century)

Chaucer was the first great poet in the English language, a
language he did so much create and shape.

> Almighty and merciable Queen,
> To whom all this world doth succour,
> To have release from sinne, sorrow and tene,
> Glorious virgin, of all the flowers, the flower,
> To thee I flee, confounded in errour.

The Well of Pity (Suffering)

Possibly the most enduring and popular hymn in English in honour of our Blessed Mother, was written by John Lingard (nineteenth century), saintly priest and very distinguished historian.

> Hail, Queen of Heaven, the ocean star, guide of the wanderer here below ... pray for the wanderer, pray for the sinner, pray for me.

The Angelus

'The Angelus' is a fourteenth century prayer in honour of the Annunciation.

> The angel of the Lord,
> Declared unto Mary,
> And she conceived by the Holy Spirit. Hail Mary,
> Behold the handmaid of the Lord,
> Be it done to me according to your word. Hail Mary,
> And the Word was made flesh,
> And dwelt among us. Hail Mary,
> Pray for us, O holy Mother of God
> That we may be made worthy of the promises of Christ.
> Let us pray:
> Pour forth, we beseech Thee O Lord,
> Thy grace into our hearts, that we,
> To whom the incarnation of Christ,
> Thy Son, was made known by the message of an angel,
> May by His Passion and Cross,
> Be brought to the glory of his Resurrection,
> Through Christ, our Lord. Amen.

In former ages the Angelus bell was heard at 6 a.m., noon, and 6 p.m.

In the ninth century, Alcuin of York, adviser to the Emperor of the West, Charlemagne the Great, at the court of Aachen (Aix-La-Chapelle; West Germany) introduced the custom of making Saturday special in honour of the Blessed Virgin, and so from the middle of the fourteenth century onwards it became the custom for people to fast on Saturdays in honour of the Blessed Virgin.

At the battle of Crécy (1346) the English soldiers went into battle without breakfast, in honour of the Blessed Virgin.

In the thirteenth century, William the Lion, King of Scotland, ordered rest from work on Saturday from noon onwards, as proof of love for the Church and the Blessed Virgin. It also allowed people the opportunity to go to confession.

At Magdalen College, Oxford, the singing of our Lady's Anthem on Saturday was one of the devotions prescribed by the founder, William of Waynflete (1395–1486).

An anthem such as the 'Salve Regina', 'Ave Maris Stella', 'Regina Caeli' or 'Alma Redemptoris Mater' was recited according to the various liturgical seasons.

Each day of the week also has its special devotion:

> Monday
> Pray for the souls in Purgatory.
>
> Tuesday
> Pray in honour of the Guardian Angels.
>
> Wednesday
> Pray in honour of St Joseph for the grace of a holy and happy death.
>
> Thursday
> Remembering the holy Eucharist in prayer.
>
> Friday
> The Passion of our Lord Jesus Christ.
>
> Saturday
> Prayers and fasting in honour of our Blessed Lady.

Good Samaritan

Copyright © John August Swanson 2002

8 September

Birthday of the Blessed Virgin Mary

et us celebrate with joyful hearts the birth of the Virgin Mary, of whom was born the Son of Justice, Christ our Lord.

Entrance Antiphon at Mass

We celebrate the Birthday of the Blessed Virgin Mary because she is the Mother of God and Mother of all peoples everywhere of whatever country, colour or language. She cherishes in her heart all migrants seeking shelter, work and security.

> Now God's home is with humankind. He will live with them and they shall be his people. God himself will be with them, and he will be their God. His name is God-with-them.

> Revelations 21:3

> You shall be holy to me; for I the Lord am holy, and have separated you from the peoples, that you should be mine.

> Leviticus 20:26

In His lifetime, Jesus honoured His Mother and foster father St Joseph. When Jesus was twelve years old and remained behind in the Temple after the Passover:

> He went down with them and came to Nazareth and lived there under their authority.

> Luke 2:51

At Cana and on Calvary He showed great reverence for His Mother.

Only one is wise, terrible in deed, seated on His throne, the Lord. He Himself created her, looked on her and assessed her to be with humankind as a gift, and He conveyed her to those who love Him.

Ecclesiasticus 1:8–10

I loved her more than health or beauty, preferred her to the light, since her radiance never sleeps.

Wisdom 7:10

She is a breath of the power of God, pure emanation of the glory of the Almighty; hence nothing impure can find a way into her. She is a reflection of the eternal light, untarnished mirror of God's active power, image of his goodness.

Wisdom 7:25–26

She deploys her strength from one end of the earth to the other, ordering all things for good.

Wisdom 8:1

In the eighth century BC, the prophet Isaiah foretold:

The maiden is with child and will soon give birth to a son,
    whom she shall call Emmanuel.

Isaiah 7:14

The angel Gabriel was most courteous:

Rejoice so highly favoured. The Lord is with you. Mary do not be afraid; you have won God's favour.

Luke 1:28–29

The Holy Spirit will come upon you and the power of the Most High will cover you with his shadow. And so the child will be called holy, and will be called Son of God.

Luke 1:35–36

Elizabeth likewise treated Mary most respectfully, called her 'blessed' and was the first to name her 'Mother of her Lord' (Luke 48).

Many feasts are celebrated in her honour, both in the month of May ('growth in everything') and October, the month of the rosary. Many churches bear her name and there are many pilgrimages to shrines such as Lourdes, Fatima, Medugorje – places where the Blessed Mother made herself known to children and young people.

> Who is this rising like the dawn, resplendent as the sun, terrible as an army in battle array?
>
> Song of Songs 6:10

For forty years, in the desert, the Hebrews carried the Ark of the Covenant with them as a focal point of the God's presence. The Ark contained tablets of the Ten Commandments and manna. Mary is the New Ark of the Covenant who bore within herself the '…living bread which came down from heaven. Come eat my bread and drink the wine I have prepared for you!' (Proverbs 9:5)

> From eternity in the beginning he created me, and for eternity I shall remain … I have taken root in a privileged people in the Lord's property, in his inheritance.
>
> Ecclesiastics 21:14–16

> Let us pray:
> Almighty, everlasting God,
> who by the co-operation of the Holy Spirit,
> prepared the body and soul of the
> glorious Virgin Mary to become a
> worthy dwelling for you Son,
> grant as we rejoice in her commemoration,
> we may by her loving intercession,
> be delivered from present evils,
> and from everlasting death,
> through Christ, our Lord. Amen.

Lord,
may your Church, renewed in this
holy Eucharist, be filled with joy
at the birth of the Virgin Mary,
who brought the dawn of hope
and salvation to the world.

Post-communion prayer

From the Divine Office for the Feast of the Birthday of the Blessed Virgin Mary

Morning Prayer

Antiphon 1

Today is the Birthday of the glorious Virgin Mary, of the seed of Abraham who rose from the tribe Judah and the stock of David.

Antiphon 2

When the sacred Virgin was born, then the world was filled with light; blessed and holy is the stock, which bore such blessed fruit.

Antiphon 3

With joy let us celebrate the nativity of Blessed Mary that she may intercede for us with the Lord Jesus Christ.

Bendictus Antiphon

Your birth, O Virgin Mother of God, announced joy to the whole world, for from you has risen the

Son of justice, Christ our God. He released us from the ancient curse and made us blessed; he destroyed death and gave us eternal life.

Short Responsary

The Lord chose her, chose her before she was born. He made her live in his own dwelling place.

Morning Intercessions

Eternal Word, in the living flesh of Mary you found a dwelling place on earth; remain with us forever in hearts free from sin.

Evening Prayer

Magnificat Antiphon

Let us remember the worthy birth of the glorious Virgin Mary.

The Lord looked on her in her lowliness and sent his angel to announce to her that she would conceive and bear the Redeemer of the world.

Scripture Reading

Who is this arising like the dawn, fair as the moon, resplendent as the sun, terrible as an army set in battle array?

Alternative Intercessions

Through the prayers of Mary, our Mother, heal the sick, comfort the sorrowful, pardon sinners; grant peace and salvation to all.

In 1644 Ralph Corby and John Duckett were both condemned to death for their priesthood. They were both very pleased when their execution was postponed to 7 September, which was the vigil of the Feast of the Blessed Virgin Mary, 8 September 1644. This made Father Corby exclaim:

> For that holy and happy Saturday which is the vigil of her glorious virginity by whose intercession I hope to be born again to a new and everlasting life.

7 September, 1644

12 September

The Most Holy Name of Mary

Throughout the Bible names are especially significant for they express the personality of the individual.

The Virgin's name was Mary.

Luke 1:27

The name Mary or Miriam in Syriac means 'sovereign Lady'; in Hebrew it means 'star of the sea'. While raised above all the saints and angels as sovereign Lady and Queen, she is also a refulgent star for all who live in our stormy world. We name Jesus as 'Our Lord', Mary as 'Our Lady'. We invoke her powerful name to beg for her continual protection.

I will make your name to be remembered to all generations; therefore shall the people praise you for ever and ever.

Psalm 45:17

St Anthony of Padua (thirteenth century) declared that 'Mary's name is sweeter than the honeycomb to the lips, sweeter than melodious music to the ear, sweeter than purest joy to the heart.'

St Bonaventure (also thirteenth century), known as the 'Seraphic Doctor' always bowed his head in reverence at Mary's name.

Throughout time Mary has been venerated as the Mother of God but also as a pure ever-virginal woman. The perfect mother, the one who begs mercy from God for all His children, who herself has experienced very deep suffering, in being witness to the most painful and humiliating death of her divine son.

Up till our own times Mary has been the object of visions, prayers and pilgrimages, and her Magnificat resounds each day in the Evening Prayer of the Divine Office.

Oxford Companion to the Bible

In the year AD 431 the Third General Council met at Ephesus (modern Turkey) and declared Mary as *Theotokos*, that is, 'God-bearer'.

St Cyril of Alexandria addressed the assembly with these soul-stirring words:

Hail Mary, thou by whom the Son of God gives light to them that sit in darkness and the shadow of death, by whom the prophets have spoken, by whom the apostles have preached salvation to the world, by whom the dead (i.e. sinners) are raised to life, by whom Kings reign! Who can give utterance to the praises of which Mary is worthy! Hail to you O Mary! Venerable treasure of the whole earth, inextinguishable Lamp of the Word, crown of virginity, sceptre of true doctrine, indissoluble temple of God, dwelling of Him whom no place can contain: Mother and Virgin, by whom He is named Blessed in the gospels, Who is come in the name of the Lord...

What tongue can worthily praise the most glorious Virgin Mary?

This Feast of the Most Holy Name of Mary follows naturally after the celebration of her birthday on 8 September. In 1683, Pope Innocent XI extended the observance of this feast to the whole universal Church in thanks giving to our Lady for the victory of the Christian forces of Jon Sobieski, King of Poland, over the Turks who were besieging Vienna and threatening to overrun the continent of Europe.

We name the Blessed Virgin as 'Our Lady' as a tribute to her heavenly inner strength and her exaltation of the humble and oppressed over the might of the powerful.

Grant we pray you, Almighty God, that your faithful people, who rejoice in the name and protection of the most holy Virgin Mary, may her maternal intercession be delivered from all evil on earth and led to the eternal joys of heaven.

We ask this, through our Lord Jesus Christ, who lives and reigns with you, in the unity of the Holy Spirit, one God for ever and ever. Amen.

Collect from the Mass of the Feast

Blessed is the womb of the Virgin Mary,
    Which bore the Son of the eternal Father.

Communion prayer

O Virgin Mother of God, He whom the whole world cannot contain, enclosed himself within your womb, being made Man

Gradual (to be said between the
epistle and the gospel)

Many daughters have succeeded virtuously; but you have surpassed them all.

Proverbs 31:29

As a lamp shining in a holy place,
    So is the beauty of age worn face.

Ecclesiastics 26:14

Dear children!
Also today, I call you to bring love where there is hatred and food where there is hunger. Open your hearts, little children, and let your hands be extended and generous, so that, through you, every creature may thank God the creator. Pray, little children, and open your hearts to God's love, but you cannot if you do not pray. Therefore pray, pray, pray. Thank you for having responded to my call.

Our Lady of Peace, Medugorje, 25 September 2004

Daniel
Copyright © John August Swanson 2000

15 September

Our Lady of Sorrows

Happy is the Blessed Virgin Mary,
   Who without dying
   Won the palm of martyrdom
   Beneath the cross of the Lord.*

Crucifixion – the nailing of a person to a tree – was considered the most cruel and most shameful method of capital punishment.

It was adopted from the East by the Romans. It was the Roman Emperor, Constantine (280–337) who eventually banned this form of lethal suffering.

All mothers feel their children's sufferings and joys with them.

The whole life of Jesus was a living sacrifice of love that embraced the scourging, the crowning with thorns, the carrying of the cross, the crucifixion. His immaculate virgin Mother felt in her heart and mind all the pains of Jesus: 'All you who pass this way, look and see; is any sorrow like the sorrow that afflicts me.' (Lamentations 1:12)

Jesus Himself was in the prime of life when He was crucified on Calvary. At much the same age, John the Baptist was beheaded at the command of Herod to please the lascivious Salome and her sinful mother. In our own times, many mothers are weeping for their children, lost to them through war-conflict, violent gang culture, drug addiction… Cut off from the healing power of love.

Simeon was a devout old man, '…waiting for the consolation of Israel…' (Luke 2:25–26)

---

* This is said before the reading of the Gospel at the Mass of Our Lady of Sorrows

When he sees the infant Jesus being brought into the temple, he gives praise for having seen God's salvation.

> As the child's father and mother stood there wondering at the things that were being said about him, Simeon blessed them and said, 'You see this child. He is destined for the fall and rising of many in Israel, destined to be a sign that is rejected – and a sword will pierce your own soul too – so that the secret thoughts of many may be revealed.
>
> Luke 2:33–35

The Mother of Jesus, in the intimacy of her life with St Joseph, must have pondered deeply in her heart the ominous words of Simeon: 'This child is set for the rise and fall of many in Israel'. When would this happen? Where? Under what form would the prediction be realized? 'A sword shall pierce your heart also'. The 'sword' must in some way include her young son, so powerless in His infancy.

Her anxiety would have increased during the years of Jesus' public life, especially her gradual awareness of the bitter opposition of the priestly hierarchy in Jerusalem.

> Near the cross stood his mother and his mother's sister, Mary the wife of Cleopas, and Mary Magdala. Seeing his mother and the disciple he loved standing near her, Jesus said to his mother, 'Woman, this is your son!' Then, to his disciple, he said, 'This is your mother.' And from that moment the disciple made a place for her in his home.
>
> John 19:25–27

The Franciscan friar, Jacaponi Di Todi (thirteenth century) composed the following very beautiful sequence:

Stabat Mater Dolorosa

At the cross her station keeping,
Stood the mournful mother weeping,
Close to Jesus at the last.

Through her soul, whose moanings low,
Told how grievous was her woe,
Sorrow like a sword had passed.

O how sad, how sorrow-laden,
Stood the meek and blessed maiden,
God's true mother undefiled!

Christ above in torment hangs,
She beneath beholds the pangs
Of her dying glorious Son.

Who is he who would not weep,
Could he know what anguish deep
Pierced the Mother of our Lord?

Who from sorrow could refrain
Gazing on that Mother's pain
Weeping with her Son adored?

She beheld the torments sore
He for His own people bore,
Bowed beneath that scourging dread.

For the sins of His own nation
She saw Him hang in desolation
Till His spirit forth He sent.

Come, O Mother, love's sweet spring,
Let me share thy sorrowing,
Let my tears unite with thine.

Let my heart be all on fire,
Still to seek with fond desire,
Christ my God, my love divine

Holy Mother pierce me through;
In my heart each wound renew
Of my Saviour crucified.

Let me share with thee His pain,
Who for all my sins was slain,
Who for me in torments died.

Let our tears in mingling tide,
Flow from Jesus crucified,
Till life cease within my breast.

By the cross with thee to stay,
There with thee to weep and pray,
Is all I ask of thee to give.

Virgin of all virgins blest;
Listen to my fond request,
Let me share thy grief divine.

The novelist Sir Walter Scott (1771–1832) admired this sequence so much that he said he would have willingly given up all his works to have written such an exquisite and beautiful lament.

Suffering is a consequence of original sin.
Suffering is a profound mystery, which when offered to Christ becomes a participation in the saving work of Christ.

Catechism of the Catholic Church, no. 1521

The Mother of Jesus shared in His suffering especially during the last week of His life, and on Calvary. We have to pray that God will give us the strength and patience to cope with suffering.

The price of mature selfless love is suffering.

Father Slavko

We must always do all we can to alleviate the suffering of others as our Lord wishes us to do.

I tell you solemnly, in so far as you did this to the least of these brothers (and sisters) of mine, you did it to me.

Matthew 25:40

107

It was the will of Christ especially to have His mother share in the redemptive passion so that she could obtain for all her children more abundant fruits of that sacrifice.

Evening Prayer for the Feast of our Lady of Sorrows from the Divine Office

God our Father,
When your Son, Jesus was raised up on the cross,
It was your will that Mary, his Mother, should
Stand there and suffer with him in her heart.
Grant that, in union with her,
The Church may share in the passion of Christ,
And so be brought to the glory of the resurrection.
We make our prayer through our Lord Jesus Christ,
Who lives and reigns with you in the unity of the
Holy Spirit, one God, for ages unending.
Amen.

24 September

Our Lady of Ransom

In our own day we use the title Our Lady of Mercy/Our Lady of Pity. For the most part we are a city-based commercial civilization, familiar with crowding, congestion and unending traffic noise. Through all this we must remember that, '...it is death to limit oneself to what is unspiritual; life and peace can only come with concern for the spiritual.' (Romans 8:6)

It is essential amid the turmoil of modern living to lead lives of prayer, and be concerned with the welfare of the world in which we live.

> Be compassionate as your Father is compassionate. Do not judge.
>
> Luke 6:36

> Feed the hungry, welcome the migrant and refugee, clothe the naked, look after the sick and those in prison. 'I tell you solemnly in so far as you neglected to do this to one of the least of these brothers of mine, you neglected to do it to me.'
>
> Matthew 25:40–46

It is surely worthy of note that never before in modern times have there been so many charitable groups and associations dedicated to give practical help to the homeless, to disaster and famine victims and other victims of human misery.

Jesus confided His mother to us as the Mother of Mercy and Pity, for it is natural for a human being to pray that God's mercy will override His justice. Mary is the embodiment of God's everlasting covenant of love.

> Can a woman forget her baby at her breast, or fail to cherish the son of her womb? Yet if even these forget, I will never forget you.
>
> Isaiah 49:15

We are our Mother Mary's children, seeking God's mercy and pardon.

God's mercy is a model for human conduct, and the all-embracing nature of God's love is made plain in three homely stories in Luke: the finding of the sheep that was lost, the finding of the lost drachma and the dramatic story of the lost son: 'Quick, bring out the best robe and put it on him … he was lost and is found.' (Luke 15:6–22)

> Let us fall into the hands of God, rather than into the hands of men.
>
> 2 Samuel 24:14

> Sing O heavens; and be joyful O earth; and break forth into singing O mountains; for the Lord has comforted his people, and will have mercy upon his afflicted.
>
> Isaiah 49:13

That many people are physically handicapped is a mystery of God's Providence: but Christ our Lord has given His divine response in the person of His most holy Mother, Mother of Mercy, Mother of Pity.

Suffering is a profoundly human condition and is rooted in the divine mystery of the wisdom and love of God.

> The mentally handicapped person has his own dignity precisely in his handicapped state. And Christ who allows mankind to put a crown on his head and says of himself, 'I am a worm not a man' has placed himself among the great tribe of handicapped people who bear a message for mankind.
>
> As people who are suffering, who demand our love and who also return our love, they are in a special way able to have a special mission in life – if only we become aware of this.
>
> Pope Benedict XVI

In holy scripture, Wisdom appears as a female figure. Mary, our Blessed Mother '…is the tree of life for those who hold her fast, those who cling to her lead happy lives.' (Proverbs 3:18)

> She is the breath of the power of God,
>> Pure emanation of the glory of the Almighty;
>> Hence nothing impure can find a way into her.
>> She is a reflection of the eternal light,
>> Untarnished mirror of God's active power,
>> Image of his goodness.

Wisdom 7:25–26

William Shakespeare (1564–1616) in his play, *The Merchant of Venice,* has a fine appreciation of the 'quality of mercy':

> The quality of mercy is not strain'd;
>> It droppeth as the gentle rain from heaven
>> Upon the place beneath. It is twice blest;
>> It blesseth him that gives and him that takes.
>> 'Tis mightiest in the mightiest; it becomes
>> The throned monarch better than his crown…
>> It is enthroned in hearts of kings;
>> It is an attribute of God himself;
>> And earthly power doth then show likest God's
>> When mercy seasons justice.

Portia, Act IV, Sc 1

> The Lord is merciful and tender-hearted,
>> He provides food for those who fear him;
>> He never forgets his covenant.

Psalm 111:4–5

Whenever the Blessed Virgin appears in the gospels she is modest, gentle, humble, compassionate, all-loving. As our spiritual Mother all that concerns us evokes her compassion, especially when we approach her as a child to its mother.

Reverend Father Frederick William Faber (1814–63) of the London Oratory had a great love of the Blessed Virgin as Mother of Mercy.

Mother of Mercy! Day by day
> My love of thee grows more and more;
> Thy gifts are strewn upon my way,
> Like sands upon the great seashore.

Though poverty and work and woe
> The masters of my life may be,
> When times are worst, who does not know
> Darkness is light, with love of thee?

But scornful men have coldly said
> Thy love was leading me from God;
> And yet in this I did but tread
> The very path my Saviour trod.

They know but little of thy worth
> Who speak these heartless words to me;
> For what did Jesus love on earth
> One half so tenderly as thee?

Jesus, when His three hours were run,
> Bequeathed thee from the Cross to me;
> And Oh, how can I love thy Son,
> Sweet Mother, if I love not thee?

> Let us pray:
> Lord God, give to your people the joy
> Of continual health in mind and body.
> With the prayers of the Virgin Mary to help us,
> Guide us through the sorrows of this life to eternal
> happiness.

> > Concluding prayer to the Litany of Our Lady

> Dear children!
> Today I invite you to do works of mercy with love
> for me and out of love for my brothers and sisters.
> Dear children, all that you do for others, do it with
> great joy and humility towards God.

I am with you and day after day I offer your sacrifices and prayers to God for the Salvation of the world.

Thank you for having responded to my call.

Our Lady of Peace, Medugorje, 25 November 1990

The Order of Our Lady of Ransom was founded by St Peter Nolasco and St Raymond Pennafort (thirteenth century) at the request of our Lady of Mercy with the aim of freeing Christian captives from the forces of Islam, Turks and Moors.

They collected alms for the release of captives, led very holy lives of hardship and even took the place of captives to allow them to be freed.

OCTOBER

MONTH OF THE HOLY ROSARY

October Aye, thou art welcome, heaven's delicious breath! When woods begin to wear the crimson leaf, And suns grow meek, and the meek suns grow brief, And the year smiles as it draws near to its death.

William Cullen Bryants (1794–1878)

The rosary from the thirteenth century onwards was a simple well-loved prayer. Henry VI, King of England, decreed that the young scholars at Eton College on the Thames should recite the rosary every day. William of Waynflete, Bishop of Winchester and Founder of Magdalen College, Oxford, enjoined the president and the Fellows to recite the rosary devoutly each day on their knees. Geoffrey Chaucer (c.1343–1400) our first great English poet, whom John Dryden (1631–1700) named as 'The well of English undefiled!' because of his establishing southern English as the literary language of our country, in the Prologue to *The Canterbury Tales*, paints a delightful portrait of the nun, a prioress, who was called Madame Englentyne. She was extremely delicate and well-mannered, and would weep if she saw a mouse caught in a trap. She fed her pet dogs with carefully chosen titbits. Chaucer concludes her portrait thus:

> ...of small coral about her arm she bore a pair of beads, gauded all with green; and there-on hung a broach of gold full sheen, On which there was first writ a crowned 'A' and after '*Amor vincit omnia*'.

The rosary is both a vocal and mental prayer and brings to our imagination the main events in the life of Jesus and Mary. The drama of our salvation unfolds in the joyful mysteries, the basis of our salvation, how it was accomplished in the sorrowful mysteries, and brought to perfection in the glorious mysteries.

'Be it done to me according to your word' was spoken on behalf of the whole human race and sealed forever the union between our human nature and Jesus, the Son of God.

Through the mysteries of the rosary the Lord Himself walks with us in our everyday normality and our Blessed Mother accompanies us in the core mysteries of our very own lives.

The late Pope John Paul II, in his Apostolic Letter 'Rosarium Virginis Mariae', gives beautiful expression to his mystical love of the Mother of God as it unfolds in the rosary.

He wrote:

> The rosary blends easily into our spiritual life. As we sit at the school of Mary we contemplate the face of Christ through the eyes of His mother in order to immerse ourselves in the contemplation of Christ who is our peace! No one has contemplated the face of Christ as Mary has.

The saintly pontiff encouraged the recitation of the rosary in the family as an effective aid in combating the arid secularism of our world today.

> The family is the primary cell of our society! The joyful mysteries lead us to discover the secret of Christian joy – the Good News of our Lord Jesus Christ, the Word made flesh, the one Saviour of the world. The rosary leads to a deeper acquaintance with Christ.

> For me to live is Christ – to die is gain.

> Philipians 1:21

> I live, now not I, but Christ lives in me.

> Galatians 2:20

115

'The centre of gravity in the Hail Mary, the hinge, as it were, which joins the two parts, is the name of "Jesus". In the second half of the Hail Mary we entrust to her maternal intercession our lives at the hour of our death. The glorification of the Trinity at the end of each decade raises our minds to heaven and in some ways to experience the joy of Tabor: "Lord is it good for us to be here." '

Luke 9:33

The beads are a symbol of the many relationships, our bond of community and fraternity which unites us to Christ. By its nature the rosary is a prayer of peace, since it consists in the contemplation of Christ, Prince of Peace. The family rosary is also a beautiful prayer to help children to grow up in love of the good and holy, and bridges the cultural distance between them and their parents. We must present the rosary to them as a prayer of love and sympathy.

Pope John Paul II

It is worthy of note that when the Blessed Virgin appeared to Bernadette at Lourdes (1858), the children of Fatima (1917) and the young people at Medugorje, she always carried a rosary with her.

Let us pray.
O God, whose only begotten Son, by his life, death and resurrection, has purchased for us the reward of eternal life: grant, we beseech thee, that meditating on these mysteries of the most holy rosary of the Blessed Virgin Mary, we may imitate what they contain, and obtain what they promise, through Jesus Christ, our Lord.

Mary is our Ordinary Resource! Let us not fear to ask her too much for her power is unlimited, and her goodness and her treasures are inexhaustible. All for Jesus through Mary, all to Mary for Jesus. Let us go to Mary as a child to its mother.

St Marcellin Champagnat 1789–1840

Dear children!
Today, I invite you to open yourselves to God, the Creator, so that He changes you. Little children, you are dear to me. I love you all and I call you to be closer to me that your love towards my immaculate heart be more fervent. I wish to renew you and lead you with my heart to the heart of Jesus, which still today suffers for you and calls you to conversion and renewal. Through you, I wish to renew the world. Comprehend, little children, that you are today the salt of the earth, and in a special way, I implore you: be converted! Thank you for having responded to my call.

Our Lady of Peace, Medugorje, 25 October 1996

21 November

Presentation of the Blessed Virgin Mary

The first question and answer in the old Penny Catechism were:

> Who made you?
>
> God made me!
>
> Why did God make you?
>
> God made me to know Him, love Him and serve Him in this world and to be happy with Him for ever in the next!

Every human being has been given this vocation: '...to know, love and serve God and to be happy with him in eternity.'

The Feast of the Blessed Virgin that we celebrate today in prayer and sacrament marks in a special way the beginning of her vocation to become the Mother of God.

Joachim and Anna consecrate their three-year-old child to the service of the Lord. The apocrypha make mention of this presentation. The apocryphal gospels contain certain anecdotes derived from primitive tradition; they are an enlargement and enrichment of what the inspired canonical gospels relate and are part of the living memory and tradition of the universal Church. This Feast was commemorated in eastern Christendom in the sixth century and in the west from the sixteenth century. The child, Mary, enters the Temple and prepares to become the servant, the 'handmaid of the Lord'.

When the disciple is ready the master will come.

Sufi proverb, eleventh century

I love the house where you dwell, and the place where your glory shines forth.

Psalm 26:8

Every human being is called to share in our blessed Lady's vocation to make Jesus better known and loved. Through our authentic lives of compassion and forgiveness we are called to be a presence, a sacrament of Christ's presence in our everyday world.

Are you not aware that your body is a temple of the Holy Spirit?

Corinthians 6:19

In due course Mary was espoused to Joseph and at the Annunciation becomes the new temple of the Word made flesh.

Each child who comes into our world is loved by the Father and is part of God's plan. An essential part of everyone's vocation is to labour to earn our daily bread and to sanctify the time that God has given us. Jesus Himself chose a carpenter to be His foster father and gave dignity to labour by His own example:

Is not this the carpenter, the son of Mary?

Mark 6:3

The Son of man himself came not to be served, but to serve and give his life as a ransom for many.

Matthew 20:28

St Paul, flogged, stoned, shipwrecked, starving and with '…my daily preoccupation … my anxiety for all the churches' (2 Corinthians 11:28) '…earned his daily bread as a tent-maker.' (Acts 20:35)

God Himself calls everyone to their special state and vocation and gives the graces necessary to fulfil that calling. Christ came into the world to redeem it and all that He said and did was directed to that end:

Did you not know that I must be about my Father's business?

Luke 2:49

Careful fulfilment of the duties of one's calling gives a person a sense of contentment, happiness and a feeling that God is with us. But God needs us, our hands, our minds, our creative abilities, our love and affection, for '…the harvest is rich but the labourers are few, so ask the Lord of the harvest to send labourers to his harvest' (Matthew 9:37).

> And when He saw the crowds He felt sorry for them because they were harassed and dejected like sheep without a shepherd.
>
> Matthew 9:36

Labour should be a form of prayer, a form of divine worship in which God is never absent.

> Teach us to count the few days that we have and so gain wisdom of heart.
>
> Psalm 90:12

The psalmist asks:

> What is man that you are mindful of him, the son of man that you should care for him? You have made him little less than a god, You have crowned him with glory and splendour.
>
> Psalm 8:4

Shakespeare's *Hamlet* has an answer:

> What a piece of work is man!
> How noble in reason! How infinite in faculties!
> In form and moving, how express and admirable!
> In action, how like an angel!
> In apprehension how like a god!
> The beauty of the world!
> The paragon of animals!
>
> *Hamlet,* Act II, Scene 2

Our vocation is to be utterly faithful to God and man and so become '…partakers of the divine nature.' (2 Peter 1:4) Charitable constant love comprises all other virtues and enfolds them all, and has many diverse forms. When the gentle, humble St Bernadette was asked by one of the older nuns in the convent of Nevers what her vocation was, she replied: 'It is to be ill.'

Love in fact is the vocation which includes all others.
It's a universe of its own, comprising all time and space.
It's eternal!

St Therese of Lisieux 1873–1897

The Daily Prayer from the Divine Office

Morning Prayer

Benedictus Antiphon

Blessed are you, Mary, because you believed that all these things which were said to you by the Lord would be fulfilled.

Evening Prayer

Antiphon

Holy Mother of God, Mary ever-virgin, temple of the Lord, sacred dwelling place of the Holy Spirit, you alone without an equal found favour with our Lord Jesus Christ.

Concluding Prayer

Lord, as we honour the memory of the Blessed Virgin Mary and seek her help, grant that we, like her, may share in the fullness of your grace. We make our prayer through our Lord Jesus Christ, who lives and reigns with you and the Holy Spirit, for ever and ever. Amen

Dear children!
This is a time of grace for the family and, therefore, I call you to a renewal of prayer. May Jesus be in the heart of your family. In prayer, learn to love everything that is holy. Imitate the lives of the saints so that they may be an incentive and teachers of the way to holiness. May every family become a witness of love in this world that is without prayer and peace. Thank you for responding to my call!

Our Lady of Peace, Medugorje, 25 October 2004

8 December

Solemnity of the Immaculate Conception

hen December days are darkening, we sometimes see snow ('the saintly veil of maiden white') come floating down in peaceful silence as we celebrate the feast of the Immaculate Conception of the Blessed Virgin Mary.

> God hurls down hailstones like crumbs. The waters are frozen at his touch; he sends forth his word and it melts them: at the breath of his mouth the waters flow.
>
> Psalm 147:17–18

This feast consists essentially in Mary's exemption from original sin. She was never in a state of separation, or alienation from God, like all other human beings are before baptism.

The grace of the Redeemer prevented her from being tainted by original sin, whereas we have been rescued from sin through the sacrament of baptism ('How beautiful you are my love, how beautiful you are' (Song of Songs 4:1) and 'You are precious in my eyes and honoured, and I love you.' (Isaiah 43:4)).

God revealed His absolute holiness to Moses:

> Take off your shoes, for the place on which you stand is holy ground. I am the God of your father, the God of Abraham, the God of Isaac, and the God of Jacob.' At this Moses covered his face, afraid to look on God.
>
> Exodus 3:15

Mary was endowed with the beauty of God's absolute holiness from the very first moment of her existence. This feast is a celebration of the beauty of holiness of our Blessed Mother, and also the holiness of countless number of people, humble in their ordinariness, living in the presence of God and sanctifying their days in prayerful active support for all those in need of a helping hand. We are all attracted by beauty, the integrity and perfection of being that pleases the senses. The harmonious unity of the whole: music, painting or any other facet of man's creative genius which leads to 'immortal longings' for unending happiness. Beauty is '...ever ancient, ever new' (St Augustine, fifth century) because God is absolute beauty, absolute goodness.

> Be holy in all that you do, since it is the Holy One who has called you and scripture says: 'Be holy, for I am holy.'
>
> Leviticus 19:2

God speaks to us through the Blessed Virgin Mary who urges to pray the daily rosary that sinners may be converted by the beauty of holiness.

> Based on the sacrament of marriage, the family is the 'domestic' church, where children learn to pray 'as the Church' and to persevere in prayer. For young children in particular, daily family prayer is the first witness of the Church's living memory as awakened patiently by the Holy Spirit.
>
> Catechism of the Catholic Church, no. 2685

This feast is also a celebration of the beauty and dignity of every human being. ('The human body is a temple of the Holy Spirit, a manifestation of divine beauty.')

> Blessed are the pure in heart. They shall see God.
>
> Matthew 5:8

> Purity requires modesty, an integral part of temperance. Modesty protects the intimate centre of the person. It means refusing to unveil what should remain hidden.

> Modesty protects the mystery of persons and their love. Modesty is decency. It inspires our choice of clothing. It is discreet.
>
> Catechism of the Catholic Church, no 2521 and no 2522

The vocation of each one of us is to be holy:

> Before the world was made, he chose us, chose us in Christ, to be holy and spotless, and to live through love in his presence.
>
> Ephesians 1:4

Holiness is a dynamic quality. It is the way of love that heals, consoles, gives encouragement, hope, light and joy and builds and strengthens family and community. A mother feeds her children with the best food she can afford. Our Blessed Mother accompanies us to the holy Eucharist: '...the living bread which has come down from heaven. Anyone who eats this bread will live for ever.' (John 6:51)

> Light dawns for the virtuous, and joy for upright hearts. Rejoice in God, you virtuous remember his holiness and praise him.
>
> Psalm 97:11

> Purest of virgins, she was to bring forth your Son, the innocent lamb who takes away our sins. You chose her from all women to be our advocate with you and our pattern of holiness.
>
> Preface of the Mass for the Feast

Intercessions from Morning & Evening Prayer from the Divine Office

> Through the prayers of Mary, our mother, heal the sick, comfort the sorrowful, pardon sinners; grant peace and salvation to all.
> You looked on the Virgin Mary and made her

the Mother of mercy. May those who are in danger experience the depth of her love.

You called Mary to be the mother in the house of Jesus and Joseph – through her prayers help all mothers to make their homes places of love and holiness.

Concluding Prayer:

We rejoice in the privilege of our Lady's Immaculate Conception, which preserved her from the stain of sin by the power of Christ's redeeming death, and prepared her to be the Mother of God. Grant that through her prayers we ourselves may come to you cleansed of all sin. We make our prayer, through our Lord Jesus Christ, who lives and reigns with you in the unity of the Holy Spirit, one God, for ever and ever. Amen.

Immaculate

Each liturgical feast calls our attention to our duty to pray that all peoples will one day enjoy the beauty of holiness for all eternity in the kingdom of heaven.

Mother, whose virgin bosom was uncrost
  With the least shade of thought to sin allied;
  Woman! above all women glorified,
  Our tainted nature's solitary boast;
  Purer than foam on central ocean tost.

'Sonnet to the Virgin', William Wordsworth (1770–1850)

Sweet Benediction in the eternal Curse!
  Veiled glory of this lampless universe!
  Thou moon beyond the clouds!
  Thou living Form Among the dead!
  Thou star above the Storm!
  Thou harmony of Nature's art!

'The Perfect Woman', Percy Bysshe Shelley (1792–1822)

And if our faith had given us nothing more than the example of all Motherhood, so mild, so merciful, so strong, so good, so patient, peaceful, loyal, pure – that were enough to prove it higher and truer than all the creeds the world had known before… for thy feet with holiness are shod.

'The Golden Legend'
Henry Wadsworth Longfellow (1807–1882)

After Christ she is the fairest gem in all of Christendom.
    Never can she be praised enough; the supreme empress
    and queen, far exalted above all nobility, wisdom and holiness.

Martin Luther (1483–1546)

In nature there's no blemish but the mind:
    none can be called deformed but the unkind.
    Virtue is beauty.

Twelfth Night, Act III, Scene 4

Beauty is truth, truth beauty – that is all Ye know on earth, and all ye need to know.

'Ode on a Grecian Urn', John Keats (1795–1821)

The moving waters at their priestlike task of pure ablution round earth's human shores.

'Bright Star', John Keats

My son, give me your heart, and all the rest shall I likewise give you.

Proverbs 23:26

Hear, O daughter, consider and incline thine ear; forget your people and your father's house; and the king will desire your beauty.

Psalm 45:9–11

'Why are you so beautiful?' asked the young visionaries of Medugorje. 'I am beautiful because I love you. If you wish to be beautiful you must love!'

As the Father has loved me, so have I loved you. This is my commandment: love one another, as I have loved you.

John 15:9–12

With all your heart honour your father, never forget the birth-pangs of your mother. Remember that you owe your birth to them; how can you repay them for what they have done for you?

Ecclesiastics 7:27–28

Dear children!
Also today, I call you to prayer, especially today when Satan wants war and hatred. I call you anew, little children; pray and fast that God may give you peace. Witness peace to every heart and be carriers of peace in this world without peace. I am with you and intercede before God for each of you. And you must not be afraid because the one who prays is not afraid of evil and has no hatred in his heart.
Thank you for having responded to my call.

Our Lady of Peace, Medugorje, 25 September 2001

12 December

Our Lady of Guadalupe

Early in the sixteenth century the Spanish general, Hernan Cortes, virtually destroyed the Indian Aztec civilisation of Mexico, and the Aztec Indians became a subjugated and powerless people. On 9 December 1531, a Saturday, a neophyte Aztec Indian, Juan Diego, was hurrying to the city of Mexico to attend holy Mass. As he crossed over the hilly ground he heard someone calling him by name. He clambered over the rocks to see who was calling and it was then that he beheld the Blessed Virgin who asked him to tell the local bishop to have a church built on that spot. Juan was not at all well received by the bishop who was very sceptical and did not want to believe him. Both on that Saturday evening and that of Sunday the Blessed Virgin appeared in the same place waiting to hear the bishop's response. It was then that the bishop ordered Juan to ask the Lady for a sign of her authenticity, for she had claimed to be the Mother of God.

On the following Monday Juan set off early to go to Mexico city to fetch a priest to attend his dying uncle. To save time, he made a detour, but the Blessed Virgin interrupted his haste. 'What road is this you are taking, my son?'

The Virgin Mother then named herself as 'Holy Mary of Guadalupe'. She assured Juan that his uncle was now cured of his illness. On that rocky terrain the holy Mother asked Juan to gather roses, but it was neither the correct place or season for roses to grow.

Juan moved to higher ground and there roses were in full bloom. He gathered them in his long cloak and returned to the Blessed Virgin who rearranged them and warned Juan to keep them untouched and unseen until he had shown them to the bishop.

After the usual delay, he was granted a meeting with the bishop and on opening his cloak the roses fell to the ground. What a surprise and shock Juan got when he saw the bishop and attendants fall to their knees in reverence. When he himself took a look he was utterly astonished to see a life-sized picture of the Virgin such as he had formerly described to the bishop. The coarsely woven material which bears the picture is as thin and open as poor sacking, all held together by weak stitching. The chief colours imprinted are deep gold in the rays and stars, blue-green on the mantle and rose on the flowered tunic. The woman represented on the sacking is the woman of the twelfth chapter of the Book of Revelation, clothed with the sun, standing on the moon, though without the crown of stars which are on the mantle itself.

The whole picture is that of the Immaculate Conception. During those early years the whole of the American continent, which stretched from Mexico to the St Lawrence river in Canada had been dedicated to our Lady of the Immaculate Conception. Since that time the Aztec Indians have held this picture in great veneration as a focus for their contemplative mystic spirit and as a bond of nationhood.

> The courage of the vanquished is the only glory of the victor.
>
> Calderón, 1600–1681

Human beings are the crown of creation and God speaks to us in many diverse ways: through other people, through the saints and above all, through the Blessed Virgin Mary.

At Guadalupe, Lourdes, Fatima, Medugorje and other shrines, our Blessed Lady has been the messenger chosen by God to convey His compassion for the poor and powerless of this world and to remind all of us that God really exists.

Our Blessed Lady is the maternal aspect of her Son's love for the poor. At the beginning of His public life Jesus declared:

> The spirit of the Lord has been given to me, for he has anointed me. He has sent me to bring the good news to the poor.
>
> Luke 4:18

In his parable of Lazarus, lying in hunger and covered with sores at the gate far from the rich man's table, Jesus is expressing His love for the poorest of the poor.

> Now the poor man dies and was carried away by angels to Abraham's bosom (heaven). The rich man pleaded 'I am in agony in these flames.'

> Luke 16:22–24

Christ is inviting us to see His presence in the poor who are His brethren. The holy Mother chooses to confide God's messages to poor innocent children: to little Bernadette at Lourdes, at Fatima, Portugal, to three small children, Lucy, Francisco and Jacinta who, like Bernadette, could neither read nor write.

In 1981 at Medugorje, the Blessed Virgin appeared to six young people. The three of them – Ivan, Marija and Vicka – continue to experience a daily apparition. The three other visionaries, Marijana, Ivanka and Jacov, receive one apparition of the Blessed Mother once each year and this will continue until death. The Blessed Mother calls herself the 'Queen of Peace' and has said she has come to testify that God really exists. She is repeatedly asking us to pray for the conversion of sinners and for fasting on bread and water on Wednesdays and Fridays. At the end of each decade of the rosary we say:

> My good Jesus, forgive us our sins, save us from the fires of hell and lead all souls to heaven, especially those in most need of your mercy.

> Dear Children,
> With great joy in my heart I thank you for all the prayers that, in these days, you offered for my intentions. Know little children that you will not regret it, neither you nor your children. God will reward you with great graces and you will soon earn eternal life. I am near you and thank all those who, through these years, have accepted my messages, have

poured them into your life and decided for holiness and peace. Thank you for having responded to my call.

Our Lady of Peace, Medugorje, 25 June 2006

Glory be to Him whose power working in us can do infinitely more that we can ask or imagine.

Ephesians 3:20

Each morning he makes me to hear, to listen like a disciple. The Lord has opened my ear.

Isaiah 50:4

You are precious in my eyes and honoured and I love you.

Isaiah 43:4

Flight in to Egypt
Copyright © John August Swanson 2002

25 DECEMBER

CHRISTMAS

The Holy Bible opens with the words: 'In the beginning God created the heavens and the earth...' and it then proceeds to give an account of the creation of the world and of man.

St John, evangelist, echoes that primeval beginning and hails the coming of the Word into our world as an altogether new beginning for all mankind: 'In the beginning was the Word: the Word was with God and the Word was God. He was with God in the beginning.' (John 1:1)

The Word is the divine presence that existed with God for all eternity and was uniquely manifested in Jesus Christ: 'The Word was made flesh and dwelt among us.' (John 1:14)

The feast and festival of Christmas is the celebration of that entirely new beginning that St John proclaims: 'The Word is life and that life was the light of men, a light that shines in the darkness, a light that darkness could not overcome.' (John 1:5)

Christmas is the celebration of that new Life and new Light, that Word that became flesh in Bethlehem of Judea.

Christmas commemorates the greatest event in world history and intimately concerns the meaning, quality and eternal destiny of our everyday living.

Preface of Christmas I

> In the wonder of the incarnation your eternal word has brought to the eyes of faith a new and radiant vision of your glory. In him we see our God made visible and so are caught up in the love of God we cannot see.

As we turn to the angel Gabriel we hear him announcing to the Virgin Mary that she has been chosen to be the Mother of Jesus, by the power of the Holy Spirit.

'I am the handmaid of the Lord, let what you have said be done to me.' And the angel left her.

Luke 1:38

Her cousin, Elizabeth, was the first to greet Mary as 'Mother of God':

Why should I be honoured with a visit from the mother of my Lord?

Luke 1:43

St Joseph would have been distressed that no one in Bethlehem was able or willing to give them shelter:

Mary's time had come to have her child and she gave birth to a son, her first-born, and wrapped him in swaddling clothes and laid him in a manger, because there was no room for them in the inn.

Luke 3:7–8

It was to ordinary working-class people, the shepherds, that the angel first broke the good news:

'Do not be afraid! Listen, I bring you news of great joy, a joy to be shared by all the people. Today, in the town of David, a saviour has been born to you; he is Christ, the Lord. And here is a sign for you: you will find a baby wrapped in swaddling clothes and lying in a manger.' And suddenly, with the angel, there was a great throng of the heavenly host, praising and singing: 'Glory to God in the highest and peace to on earth to men of good will.'

Luke 2:10–14

The angels were not able to remain silent.

> Everyone was astonished at what the shepherds had to say, but as for Mary, she treasured all these things and pondered them in her heart. And the shepherds went back glorifying and praising God for all they had heard and seen; it was exactly as they had been told.

Luke 2:19–20

Preface of Christmas II

> Today you fill our hearts with joy as we recognise in Christ the revelation of your love. No eye can see his glory as our God, yet now he is seen as one like us. Christ is your Son before all ages, yet now he is born in time. He has come to lift all things up to himself, to restore unity to creation, and to lead mankind from exile into your heavenly kingdom.

The shepherds as representatives of the Jewish nation were not the only ones to be favoured with the Good News of the Saviour's birth. Away in southern Arabia, in Seba and Sheba (now Yemen and Oman), three very rich gentile astronomers caught a glimpse of a very brilliant new star. They resolved to follow its course because it heralded something mysterious and wonderful.

After leaving the wily King Herod they set out.

> And there in front of them was the star they had seen rising; it went forward and halted above the place where the child was. The sight of the star filled them with delight and, going into the dwelling, they saw the Child with his Mother Mary, and falling on their knees they did him homage. Then, opening their treasures they offered him gifts of gold, frankincense and myrrh. But they were warned in a dream not to go back to Herod, and returned to their own country by a different way.

Matthew 2:9–12

The gifts were symbolic: gold for a king, frankincense for God and myrrh for His manhood.

Later tradition gives the three Magi names as Gaspar, Balthazar and Melchior.

Preface of Christmas III

> Today in him a new light has dawned upon the world. God has become one with man, and man has become one again with God. Your eternal Word has taken upon himself our human weakness, giving our mortal nature immortal value. So marvellous is this oneness between God and man that in Christ man restores to man the gift of everlasting life.

In our affluent and very secular western world we are in danger of missing the depth of meaning in the mystery of Christmas. The mystery of Christmas is all about our family and love.

> Through love we become beautiful; everything is possible through love. Love turns everything to good and recognizes in every person a person it can love. The way of love is the way of real life. Love creates togetherness. Love can achieve the impossible. Love is the most beautiful gift we can offer to anyone.

> Father Slavko, 'In the School of Love'

> The love of God consists in taking trouble for one another.

> St Pachomius, fourth century

When children know and feel that they are truly loved by their parents they feel happy and secure and are well prepared for adult life. Their first impressions last the longest. Their imaginations are fired and glow when they see the crib and sing the well-known simple traditional Christmas carols. This creates a never-to-be-forgotten profound impression on them. Love can give them knowledge beyond reason, a perception of the mystery of divine love which reveals itself to love alone. Holy Mass is the mystery of the eternal order manifested in time. The sacred liturgy of holy Mass is a means of introducing our children to participate in the sublime Eucharistic mystery and so share in the divine life. Christmas celebrates the greatest event in human history and we must not trivialize and demean this feast by ignoring its true meaning.

> Dear Children,
> This is a time of great graces, but also a time of great trials for all those who desire to follow the way of peace. Because of that, little children, I again call you to pray, pray, pray, not with words but with the heart. Love my messages and be converted. Be conscious of this gift that God has permitted me to be with you, especially today, when I have little Jesus – the King of Peace – in my arms. I desire to give you peace, and that you carry it in your hearts, and give it to others until God's peace begins to rule the world. Thank you for having responded to my call.

Our Lady of Peace, Medugorje, 25 December 2002

Jesus was born in Bethlehem, a word that means 'house of bread'. Jesus is the eternal priest.

> I am the living bread which has come down from heaven.
> Anyone who eats this bread will live for ever;
> and the bread that I shall give
> is my flesh, for the life of the world.

John 6:51

To become a child in relation to God is the condition for entering the kingdom.

Matthew 18:3

For this we must humble ourselves and become little. Even more, to become 'children of God' we must be born 'from above' or 'born of God'. Only when Christ is formed in us will the mystery of Christmas be fulfilled in us. Christmas is the mystery of this marvellous exchange.

Catechism of the Catholic Church, no. 526

O marvellous exchange: man's creator has become man, born of the Virgin. We have been made sharers in the divinity of Christ, who humbled himself to share our humanity.

Antiphon 1 of Evening Prayer in the Divine Office, 1 January

No one, whether shepherd or wise man can approach God here below except by kneeling before the manger at Bethlehem and adoring him hidden in the weakness of a new-born child.

Catechism of the Catholic Church, no. 563

By his obedience to Mary and Joseph as well as by his humble work during the long years in Nazareth, Jesus gives us the example of holiness in the daily life of family and work.

Catechism of the Catholic Church, no. 564

A noble flower of Judah from tender roots has sprung
    A rose from stem of Jesse, as prophets long and sung,
    A blossom fair and bright,
    That in the midst of winter will
    Change to dawn our night.
    The rose of grace and beauty of which Isaiah sings
    Is Mary, Virgin Mother and Christ the flower she brings.
    By God's divine decree
    She bore our loving Saviour, who died to set us free.
    To Mary, dearest Mother, with fervent hearts we pray:
    Grant that your tender infant will cast our sins away,
    And guide us with his love
    That we shall ever serve him and live
    With him above.

'Es ist ein Ros', German carol, fifteenth century

OUR LADY OF FATIMA

FATIMA: COVA DA IRIA, CENTRAL PORTUGAL

he Blessed Virgin appeared six times between 13 May and October of 1917, to three shepherd children: Lucia aged ten, Francisco aged nine, and Jacinta aged seven.

They saw Our Blessed Lady brighter than the sun, standing on a cloud above an evergreen tree.

Francisco saw her, but did not hear what she said. The Lady told the children to return to the same place on the thirteenth of each month until October, when she would let them know who she was and tell them what she desired.

But beforehand, in the late Spring of 1916, an angel appeared to them and told the children: 'Pray with me. I am the Angel of Peace. Pray for unbelievers!'

The civil authorities were extremely hostile to the children, but as the thirteenth of each month approached, the crowds increased each time.

On 13 October, 1917, the day began very wet and dismal. Despite this, about 70,000 people had gathered. Our Lady told the children: 'I am Our Lady of the Rosary. I want a chapel built here. The rosary must be said every day here.' Then the sun began to 'dance', three times during a period of ten minutes. The crowd were overcome by astonishment and fear.

Our Lady told the children that people must say the rosary for peace and for the conversion of sinners. There was a kind of reflection of the 'dance' of the sun as far away as Gibraltar, Eastern France, Germany, Austria, and the Alpine peaks.

Our Blessed Lady told the children: 'Jesus wishes to use you to make me known and loved. He desires to establish devotion to my Immaculate Heart throughout the world.' She also asked for prayer to be offered for the conversion of communist Russia. We used to pray to Our Blessed Lady and the archangel, Michael, after holy Mass for this same intention.

Lucia was given, very briefly, a sighting of hell and the torments of the damned. Our Blessed Lady asked that the first Saturday of each new month should be a day of prayer and reparation for the conversion of sinners.

Our Blessed Lady also told the children to say after each decade of the rosary:

> O, my good Jesus, forgive us our sins, save us from the fires of hell, and lead all souls to heaven, especially those in most need of your mercy.

Francisco died from flu in 1918, and Jacinta too, in 1919. Lucia entered Carmel in 1948. Lucia was to reveal that:

> The sins which send most people to hell are the sins of impurity. There will be fashions in clothes, which will greatly offend Our Lord. The Church has no fashions. Our Lord is always the same.

She also said that Our Lord told her:

> All that God wishes in the way of mortification is the simple faithful performance of one's everyday tasks and the acceptance of their difficulties and hardships. The sacrifice that each one can make is to do one's duty and obey my Law. That is the kind of penance that pleases me.

The messages of our Blessed Lady at Lourdes, Fatima, Medugorje, is to pray incessantly for the conversion of sinners, and to do penance in reparation for the sins of the world.

At Medugorje, Our Lady, Queen of Peace, asks for fasting on bread and water on Wednesday and Friday of each week, for the conversion of sinners.

> Dear Children!
> Today, I call you to fill your day with short and ardent prayers. When you pray, your heart is open

and God loves you with a special love and gives you special graces. Therefore make good use of this time of grace and devote it to God more than ever. Do novenas of fasting and renunciation so that Satan be far from you and grace surround you. I am near you and intercede before God for each of you. Thank you for having responded to my call.

Our Lady of Peace, Medugorje, 25 July 2005

The ornament of a sweet and gentle disposition – this is what is precious in the sight of God.

1 Peter 3:4

Bibliography

Catechism of the Catholic Church, 1995

Catholic Encyclopaedia, 1967

R Clarke and F Spirago, *Catechism Explained,* USA, Benziger Brothers, 1927

RGS, *My Queen and My Mother,* Washbourne Ltd

P J Chandlery, *Mary's Praise on Every Tongue,* Manresa Press, 1924

Beevers, John, *Our Lady of Fatima,* St Paul Publications, 1958

L Lovesik, *Our Lady in Catholic Life*, SVD

Saint Bernadette Soubirous, *Abbé Francois Trochu*, Tan Inc., 1957